QUESTIONS & ANSWERS:
Property

Multiple Choice and Short Answer
Questions and Answers

By

JOHN COPELAND NAGLE
Professor
Notre Dame Law School

LexisNexis™

Editorial Offices
744 Broad Street, Newark, NJ 07102 (973) 820-2000
201 Mission St., San Francisco, CA 94105-1831 (415) 908-3200
701 East Water Street, Charlottesville, VA 22902-7587 (804) 972-7600
www.lexis.com

(Pub.3178)

DEDICATION

For Laura and Julia, who are learning what property is really all about.

ABOUT THE AUTHOR

John Copeland Nagle is a Professor at the Notre Dame Law School, where he teaches property, legislation, and a variety of environmental law courses. He is the co-author of "The Law of Biodiversity and Ecosystem Management," the first book designed for courses studying how the law addresses biodiversity. He is also co-authoring a forthcoming property law casebook and a book comparing environmental pollution, cultural pollution, and other kinds of "pollution." He has lectured on property, legislation, and environmental issues at numerous forums in the United States, Canada, China, and Hungary. He served as a Distinguished Lecturer at the Tsinghua University School of Law in Beijing during 2002, where he taught property law and environmental law.

Prior to joining the Notre Dame faculty, Professor Nagle was an associate professor at the Seton Hall University School of Law from 1994 through 1998. He also worked in the United States Department of Justice, first as an attorney in the Office of Legal Counsel where he advised other executive branch agencies on a variety of constitutional and statutory issues, and later as a trial attorney conducting environmental litigation. Professor Nagle served as a law clerk to Judge Deanell Reece Tacha of the United States Court of Appeals for the Tenth Circuit, and he was a scientific assistant in the Energy and Environmental Systems Division of Argonne National Laboratory. He is a graduate of Indiana University and the University of Michigan Law School.

PREFACE

Property law has a reputation for being the most difficult of the courses encountered in the first year of law school. That reputation is well earned, for the intricacies of such longstanding common law doctrines as the Rule against Perpetuities have confounded generations of law students, lawyers, judges, and professors. But much of property law relies upon the application of contemporary policies to our rapidly developing societies. An effective property law course will teach both the old rules and the new policies. This book is designed to achieve that goal, too.

This book contains questions and answers. Its primary purpose is to help you test your knowledge of the full range of property law concepts and to apply that knowledge to particular situations. Some of those situations are real, as indicated by the cases cited in the answers. Other cases are hypothetical, yet they should illustrate the problems addressed by property law equally well. The questions take two forms: short answer questions and multiple choice questions. Each of the short answer questions is designed to be answered in between five and ten minutes. The multiple choice questions should be answered in about two minutes each. The practice final exam, therefore, should take about 180 minutes to complete. But it is also important to take the time to answer every question as carefully as possible, even if that requires more time than the suggested guidelines. The point, after all, is to test your knowledge of property law, and to identify those areas where further study is needed.

I am grateful to LEXIS for publishing this valuable series of books, to Tim Zinnecker for excellent editorial advice, and to my students who continue to teach me about property law.

Professor John Copeland Nagle
Notre Dame, Indiana
May, 2003

TABLE OF CONTENTS

Page

ABOUT THE AUTHOR v
PREFACE vii

QUESTIONS 1
TOPIC 1. The Nature of Property Rights 3
TOPIC 2. Personal Property 7
TOPIC 3. Humans, Animals, and Intellectual Property 13
TOPIC 4. Estates in Land 17
TOPIC 5. Concurrent Owners 23
TOPIC 6. Landlords, Tenants, and Housing 27
TOPIC 7. Title, Ownership, and Possession 35
TOPIC 8. Private Land Use Restrictions 39
TOPIC 9. Government Land Use Restrictions 47
TOPIC 10. Takings 53
Practice Final Exam 59

ANSWERS 77
TOPIC 1. The Nature of Property Rights 79
TOPIC 2. Personal Property 83
TOPIC 3. Humans, Animals, and Intellectual Property 89
TOPIC 4. Estates in Land 93
TOPIC 5. Concurrent Owners 99
TOPIC 6. Landlords, Tenants, and Housing 103
TOPIC 7. Title, Ownership, and Possession 111
TOPIC 8. Private Land Use Restrictions 115
TOPIC 9. Government Land Use Restrictions 123
TOPIC 10. Takings 131
Practice Final Exam 137

INDEX 153

QUESTIONS

1. According to the Restatement of Property, "property" refers to "legal relations between persons with respect to a thing." How does that definition differ from the more colloquial understanding of property as "something that we own?"

ANSWER:

2. In what ways is one's vote for President property, and in what ways is it not property?

ANSWER:

3. Which of the following rules best illustrates the application of the occupation theory of property?

    (A) A riparian landowner does not own land created by avulsion.

    (B) An actress has a right to publicity that allows her to decide whether or not to exploit her celebrity for commercial gain.

    (C) A wife has a right to share in the income that her husband earned during their marriage if the couple gets divorced.

    (D) A finder gets to keep a car that has been abandoned.

4. Which of the following properties provides an example of an anticommons?

    (A) Federally owned lands that are open to the public for recreational uses.

    (B) A common interest community that requires unanimous consent to act.

    (C) A wedding ring.

    (D) A seventeenth century shipwreck that is discovered at the bottom of the Atlantic Ocean.

5. What is the most likely source of a prohibition on a casino's right to exclude a patron who is counting cards at the blackjack table?

    (A) The traditional common law limits upon public accommodations.

    (B) Local zoning ordinances.

    (C) State gaming regulations.

    (D) Federal civil rights laws.

6. Which property law or doctrine best exemplifies the labor theory of property?

    (A) The common law rules of finders.

    (B) Municipal prohibitions on spot zoning.

    (C) State anti-dilution trademark statutes.

    (D) The federal Wilderness Act.

7. Which of the following legal doctrines finds the most support from the scriptural indication that landowners should be willing to let others use their land?

    (A) Tenancies at sufferance.

    (B) The public trust doctrine.

    (C) The touch and concern requirement.

    (D) Spot zoning prohibitions.

8. The Visual Artists Rights Act of 1990 illustrates:

    (A) The role of natural rights in determining property.

    (B) The primary authority of landowners with respect to property.

    (C) The constitutional direction that intellectual property rights be of a limited duration.

    (D) The unwillingness of the law to make judgments about artistic value.

9. The aphorism that "possession is nine-tenths of the law" is best disproved by the law of:

    (A) Avulsion.

    (B) Accretion.

    (C) Accession.

    (D) Adverse possession.

The Coopers live in a sparsely populated, mountainous county with no zoning laws. They have a mountain lion that they keep as a pet. A county ordinance allows any animal to be kept as a pet provided that the owner obtains a permit. The Coopers do not have a permit, but they would seek one if the lion ever hurt anyone. Mr. Cooper worked as a tenured professor in the local state university until his supervisor discovered that the Coopers had been keeping the mountain lion. The university administrator was not satisfied with Cooper's explanation, so he fired Cooper from his job. Cooper then applied for a job in the county public defender's office, but they declined to hire him because of the stigma associated with the mountain lion episode. Next, Cooper filed for unemployment benefits that had just been created under a new state statute, but the benefits were denied because that office, too, had heard of the Coopers' trouble with the mountain lion. Finally, the county confiscated the mountain lion.

10. Which of the following constitutes property that the government cannot take from the Coopers without due process of law?

   (A)   The job as a professor. *gov. job*

   (B)   The job in the state public defender's office.

   (C)   The unemployment benefits.

   (D)   The pet mountain lion.

Nineteenth century American statesman Henry Clay once wrote, "That is property which the law declares to be property."

11. Clay's definition best illustrates which theory of property?

   (A)   Natural rights theory.

   (B)   Utilitarian theory.

   (C)   Labor theory.

   (D)   Economic theory.

12. Which type of property law provides the least protection to the right to exclude?

   (A)   The federal trademark act.

   (B)   State riparian rights to water.

   (C)   State public accommodations statutes.

   (D)   Municipal historic preservation ordinances.

On a snowy night in February 1946, Bennie Ferrone attended the premier of the movie "It's a Wonderful Life" at the Lombard Theater. She loved the movie, but her joy disappeared a couple of days later when she realized that she could not find her wallet. She looked around the house and asked her children if they had seen it, but when she could not find it, she just shrugged her shoulders and assumed that it must have fallen out of her purse somewhere. Bennie died in 1982, devising all of her property to her son Werner. In February 1999, Werner received an e-mail from Larry Cucumber, an actor who explained that he had found the wallet behind a staircase in the Lombard Theater. Vegetable Productions, Inc. (VPI), was renovating the theater for use as a movie production studio. At the time Larry found the wallet, VPI was giving him a tour of the facility in the hope that he would agree to perform in a children's movie that the company was producing. The wallet contained a driver's license that had expired in 1949, a picture of Bennie's family, and four rare postage stamps. The stamps form an intact "plate block," which consists of the four stamps and a printed number along the border. The plate block is now estimated to be worth $100,000; each stamp individually is worth about $15,000. Now Werner, Larry, and VPI all insist that they own the stamps.

13. According to the law, who is right?

ANSWER:

Ferdinand Hotz is a jeweler who made a large sapphire and diamond ring for Mr. Peet. Sometime later, the ring lost one of its diamonds, so Peet contacted Hotz to replace the diamond and repair the ring. Hotz instructed Peet to leave the ring at the St. Paul Hotel, where Hotz worked while he was in town. Peet went to the hotel and explained that he wanted to leave the ring for Hotz, and he watched the hotel's cashier put the ring in an envelope marked "Ferdinand Hotz." But Hotz never made it to the hotel that day because he was detained out-of-town. In fact, a month passed until Hotz returned to the hotel, and it was only then that he learned that Peet had left the ring for him at the hotel one month before. The ring was apparently stolen by an unknown thief after the hotel's cashier placed the marked envelope on the counter right after Peet gave it to her.

14. Can Peet recover the value of the ring from the hotel?

ANSWER:

Arthur just took the bar exam. He is sure that he has failed. So sure, in fact, that he tells his classmate Charlie that Charlie can have the new laptop that Arthur planned to use in his law practice. Arthur explains that the laptop is being shipped from the manufacturer and should arrive at his home in three days. One day later, though, Arthur is killed in a car accident. Charlie asks Arthur's heirs for the laptop, but they refuse to give it to him.

15. Does Charlie own the laptop?

ANSWER:

Eddie proposes to Brenda. She agrees to marry him, and he gives her a $10,000 diamond engagement ring. Six months later, and just three days before the wedding, Eddie decides that he would rather marry Alice instead. Eddie asks Brenda to return the ring, but she refuses.

16. Why should Brenda be able to keep the ring?

ANSWER:

17. Some courts have rejected the traditional common law rule governing treasure troves because that rule:

(A) Encourages trespassers.

(B) Discourages finders.

(C) Rewards passive landowners.

(D) Contradicts the law of adverse possession.

18. A landowner will be able to keep which property that has been found at her home?

(A) A ring that a houseguest accidentally left beside the swimming pool and that was discovered by another guest the next day.

(B) $10,500 found by a tenant in a pail on a basement shelf, and who advertised that find in the local newspaper for the statutorily mandated ninety days. *mislaid*

(C) A basketball that bounced onto her driveway while the neighborhood kids were playing next door.

(D) A bald eagle that was electrocuted by a power line and fell dead onto her backyard.

Victor proposes to Mary, who quickly agrees to marry him. Victor tells Mary that there is a beautiful diamond engagement ring waiting for her at the local jewelry store. But Victor is so excited that he fails to pay attention as they are driving to the store, and he crashes into an oncoming truck. Mary is unhurt, but Victor is killed. Mary wants the ring to remember Victor by, but Victor's heirs object.

19. Mary will:

(A) Get the ring as an inter vivos gift.

(B) Get the ring as a gift causa mortis.

(C) Get the ring according to either an inter vivos gift or gift causa mortis theory.

(D) Not get the ring under either theory.

Conrad is the world's leading collector of first edition books written by Mark Twain. Cary steals a rare copy of Twain's book *Roughing It* from the library in Conrad's estate in the Hamptons. Two weeks later and thousands of miles away, Cary walks into the City Book Store with the book and a letter purporting to be from Conrad. The letter states that "I would like to exchange this copy of *Roughing It* for your copy of *A Connecticut Yankee in King Arthur's Court*, which is the last book that I need to complete my collection of all of Twain's works. My book has been appraised for twice the value of your book, so I hope you will agree to this transaction." The note is signed "Conrad," though it was actually forged by Cary. The proprietor of the City Book Store is also impressed with Cary's knowledge of Conrad's collection, facts that Cary learned both by reviewing Conrad's web site and by Cary's personal observation while stealing the book. Cary thus swaps books with the City Book Store. Two hours later, Cary returns to his own antiques store and sells the copy of *A Connecticut Yankee in King Arthur's Court* to Isabella.

20. Who owns the copy of *A Connecticut Yankee in King Arthur's Court?*

(A) Conrad.

(B) Cary.

(C) The City Book Store.

(D) Isabella.

21. If the facts in Question 20 are the same except that Conrad gave the copy of *Roughing It* to Cary instead of Cary stealing it, who owns the copy of *A Connecticut Yankee in King Arthur's Court?*

(A) Conrad.

(B) Cary.

(C) The City Book Store.

(D) Isabella.

Roberto Rancher owns 500 acres of mountainous, arid land in Arizona along the Mexican border. One day, while he is looking for a lost cow, he discovers a small valley that he had never seen before. He soon spots a sport utility vehicle crashed at the bottom of the valley. The SUV is marked "Desert Tours," and the only thing inside is a bag sitting on the front seat that is filled with $24,000 in U.S. currency. Rancher reports his find to Desert Tours, who explains that the SUV had been stolen seven months before. Desert Tours has no idea where the money came from but says that it should get the money now.

22. Whether Rancher or Desert Tours gets the money found in the SUV depends upon whether that money is viewed as:

(A) Lost or mislaid.

(B) Mislaid or abandoned.

(C) Abandoned or a treasure trove.

(D) Lost or abandoned.

23. Which of the following is personal property?

(A) A copyrighted book on the wines of California.

(B) The idea for a new procedure for cultivating grapes. *IP*

(C) A newly planted vineyard. *RP*

(D) The building housing a winery's restaurant. *RP*

Claude Campisi pays $100 to dock his boat in the Seaside Marina early one morning. The marina gives him a swipe card that allows him to reenter the gate to the marina. Campisi goes out to lunch, visits his friends, and then realizes that he has lost his wallet, the swipe key contained in it, and his boat keys. So Campisi returns to the marina to see if the marina's employees can start the boat for him, but the boat is gone.

24. Campisi's lawsuit against the marina will likely:

(A) Succeed because the marina was grossly negligent.

(B) Succeed because the marina was negligent.

(C) Fail because the marina was not negligent.

(D) Fail because the marina was not grossly negligent.

25. The establishment of an online international database that contains a comprehensive inventory of all artwork that has been reported as stolen around the world will most influence the rules governing:

(A) Adverse possession.

(B) Bailments.

(C) Finders.

(D) Gifts.

Samuel wants to thank Kelly, his employee, for landing a lucrative government contract. Samuel thus writes a letter stating as follows: "In recognition of extraordinary effort, I am hereby giving Kelly my antique quill pen that was once used by Thomas Jefferson." The pen itself, Samuel explains, was on display in the building's lobby, and he tells Kelly to meet him in his office tomorrow morning to receive the pen itself. One of Kelly's colleagues, Omar, overhears the conversation and enters Samuel's office after Kelly leaves. "Thomas Jefferson is a distant relative," Omar explains to Samuel, "and I will pay you $50,000 for that pen." Samuel agrees, accepts Omar's check for $50,000, and promises to give him the pen tomorrow morning. The next morning, Kelly arrives early and explains his situation to the building's custodian, who then opens the display case and gives Kelly the pen.

26.   Who owns the pen?

(A)   Samuel.

(B)   Kelly.

(C)   Omar.

(D)   Thomas Jefferson's heirs.

Jeff is a law student whose laptop computer is broken. He takes the computer to We Fix It, a local store that is popular with students both because of its ability to solve any computer problem and because it offers used computers for sale at low prices. Two days later, Monica sees the computer on display at We Fix It and buys it. Monica did not know that the computer was Jeff's until she brings it home from the store and a mutual friend recognizes the picture of Jeff's family that serves as the wallpaper for the computer.

27.   Who owns the computer?

(A)   Jeff, because he was the original owner.

(B)   Jeff, because We Fix It did not act in good faith.

(C)   Monica, because We Fix It had voidable title.

(D)   Monica, because We Fix It has void title.

H.M. Chaney owns a $23,514.70 certificate of deposit. When he became sick, he wrote the following on the back of the certificate: "Pay to Martin, but not until my death. My life seems to be uncertain. I may live through this spell. Then I will attend to it myself." Chaney delivers the certificate to Martin and dies two weeks later without recovering from his sickness.

28.   Martin's suit to cash the certificate will:

(A)   Succeed, because it is a valid gift causa mortis.

(B)   Succeed, because Chaney actually delivered the certificate to Martin.

(C)   Fail, because the death of the donor cannot be a precondition to the validity of the gift.

(D)   Fail, because Chaney did not satisfy the delivery requirement.

29.   Which business is most likely to be liable to Julia if it loses the goods that she left with it?

(A)   You Park It, which allowed Julia to park her car on its land near the airport.

(B)   The First National Bank, which kept Julia's antique watch in a safe deposit box.

(C)   Jose's Parking Lot, which allowed Julia to park her car in its enclosed garage without knowing that she had an expensive Ming dynasty vase in a box in the trunk.

(D) The Hillis Department Store, where Julia accidentally left her purse containing $2,000 in cash.

30. According to a utilitarian theory of property, why should there be no property in human slaves?

ANSWER:

The First National Bank of Denver was founded in 1876, at the height of the Colorado silver boom. It became the leading bank in the state for over a century. Then, in the 1980's, the bank began to expand throughout the Rocky Mountain region. To demonstrate its new regional presence, the bank decides that it wants to change its name to First Interstate Bank. Residents of Denver are soon greeted with television advertisements, billboards, and newspaper stories proclaiming that "The days of the First National Bank of Denver are behind us; come visit the new First Interstate Bank." The day of the change features numerous celebrations at the bank's headquarters and throughout Denver. Two weeks later, a small bank on the outskirts of Denver announces that it is changing its name from Suburban Bank to the First National Bank of Denver.

31. Can the original First National Bank of Denver — now called First Interstate — block Suburban Bank from adopting its new name?

ANSWER:

32. Why is a physician exempt from a conversion claim when she removes body parts from a patient during a routine surgical procedure and then keeps them for later use in medical research?

ANSWER:

A wolverine is a fierce predator that lives in forests in Michigan and elsewhere. Wolverines are not common, but they are not protected by federal law. A family of wolverines lives on the forested property of the UP Timber Company in northern Michigan. UP has given permission to Nancy Naturalist, a local photographer, to come onto its lands to photograph the wolverines, and the animals have become so comfortable with Nancy that they sit still while she photographs them from as close as ten feet away. The Michigan Zoo wants to buy the wolverines that Nancy has been photographing so that the zoo can feature them in a new exhibit of native animals.

33. Who does the zoo have to pay to acquire those wolverines?

(A) UP.

(B) Nancy.

(C) The State of Michigan.

X (D) No one.

34. Which of the following can be copyrighted?

(A) Your name.

(B) The recipe that you have memorized for making chocolate chip cookies.

X (C) Your wedding video.

(D) The directions that you give over the phone to your private mountain retreat.

35. Courts have applied the term "quasi property" to:

X (A) Dead bodies and news.

(B) Human genes and trade secrets.

(C) Dead bodies and trade secrets.

(D) Human genes and news.

36. Which of the following *cannot* be patented?

(A) The sunsy, a new plant created by Acme Nurseries that is a hybrid between a sunflower and a daisy.

(B) The manufacturing process employed by Bigger Nurseries — Acme's leading competitor — to produce a synthetic sunsy.

(C) The Sunsymatic, the machine that Bigger Nurseries uses to make its synthetic sunsies.

X (D) The genes that Acme Medical Research, Inc., takes from a field of pecos sunflowers in New Mexico for use as a treatment for diabetes.

37. Thelma lawfully owns:

(A) A deer that visits her garden every night.

(B) A pet deer that escapes from her neighbor's land and which Thelma captures and refuses to return. *not wild — can't capture*

(C) A Florida Key deer which is listed under the federal Endangered Species Act and which Thelma captures.

X (D) The exclusive rights to use her drawing of a smiling Florida Key deer to identify the chain of hotels that she operates in southern Florida.

38. Intellectual property rights are designed to:

    (A) Combat monopolies.

    (B) Encourage creators.

    (C) Discourage harmful speech.

    (D) Diminish the importance of land ownership.

The Danish band Aqua records the song "Barbie Doll," which soon becomes an international hit. Alas, Mattel — the toy manufacturer that produces Barbie dolls — is not amused.

39.   Mattel fails to block Aqua from performing the song in concert, though, for each reason *except*:

    (A) The copyright law does not apply to live performances.

    (B) The song does not constitute trademark infringement because it does not suggest that it is created by Mattel.

    (C) The first amendment restricts government regulation of the song because the song is not purely commercial speech.

    (D) The song satisfies the noncommercial use exception of the Federal Trademark Dilution Act.

40.   Commercial sperm banks are subject to little government regulation because:

    (A) Human body parts cannot be treated as property.

    (B) The state's police power may not be employed to regulate any aspects of human reproduction.

    (C) Few state legislatures have approved such regulation.

    (D) Any public concerns about such facilities are adequately addressed by private consensual agreements between the facilities and the donors.

41.   The "fair use" provision of the federal copyright act presumes that:

    (A) Ideas cannot become property.

    (B) Monopoly power over written works is contrary to the public interest.

    (C) There is a natural right to use written works for noncommercial purposes.

    (D) Written works retain their commercial value for a short period of time.

In 1986, Amy conveyed 200 acres of prime New Campbell beachfront property to Babs "so long as the property is used for a vacation home for the next 40 years." The area consists of dozens of vacation homes at the time of the conveyance, but since then most of the other vacation homes have been replaced by commercial development. Earlier this year Babs held a press conference to announce her plans to build a shopping mall.

42.   What will happen if she tries to do so?   *fs det.*

ANSWER:

Sheila wants to help provide for her godson Chris, but she does not think he will need any financial assistance if he becomes a doctor. So Sheila conveys her valuable lake house in South Coleman "to Chris for life or until he graduates from medical school."

43.   Who owns what interest in the house?   *le det   fer s
poss rev.*

ANSWER:

In 2002, Stewart conveyed his townhouse in New Campbell "to Alice's children who reach the age of 30." Alice died in 1999, survived by her son Larry (who was born in 1997) and her daughter Melinda (who was born in 1983). It is now 2003.

44.   Who owns what interest in the townhouse?

ANSWER:

Pat married in 1959. She later had three children: John was born in 1960, Jim in 1962, and Susan in 1965. In 1971, Pat wrote a will devising her farm in New Campbell "to all of my grandchildren born within the next 40 years." When Pat dies in 2001, she is survived by her husband Jim and by her three children, but she does not have any grandchildren.

45.   Who owns what interest in the farm?

ANSWER:

Oscar conveys his beachfront property "to Anne for life, then to Barbara, but if Barbara marries before Anne dies, then to Christine."

46. Who owns what interest in the property?

ANSWER:

Acme Pharmaceuticals owns two lots next to its headquarters in downtown Metropolis. No buildings stand on the lots, and for several decades Acme has encouraged the public to use the land for picnics and recreational purposes. Acme has to dispose of the land because of the property tax burden, but the company does not want the public to lose the opportunity to use the land. The only willing buyer was Isaac Investor. Accordingly, Acme sells the two lots "to Isaac for life, but if the property is ever used commercially, then to the City of Metropolis."

47. Who owns what interest in the land?

ANSWER:

On March 1, 1999, Julia conveyed ten acres of land "to Gloria for life." On March 2, Julia conveyed her entire remaining interest to Sydney and her heirs.

48. Who owns what interest in the ten acres of land?

ANSWER:

Lisa conveys her home "to Irene for life and then to Brandi and her heirs if Brandi is 21 years old before Irene dies, or to Cherrie and her heirs if Brandi is not 21 before Irene dies."

49. Who owns what interest in the home?

ANSWER:

Reverend Thomas Sutton sells a chicken farm on the outskirts of a developing urban area "to Archibald Campbell, but if any gambling is permitted on the property within 21 years of the death of any child of Archibald's born before Reverend Sutton's death, then to James Edwin."

50. Who owns what interest in the land?

ANSWER:

PLIES Incorporated conveys its valuable downtown property "to Ken for life, then to Ken's widow for life, and then 30 years after the termination of the last life estate, to Marci for life." *cr le*   *cr le*

51.   Who owns what interest in the land?

ANSWER:

In 1990, Celia wrote a will devising all of her property "to Andrew for life, then to the children of Andrew for life, and upon the death of the last surviving child of Andrew, to such of Andrew's grandchildren as may then be living." Celia dies in 2000, when Andrew and his daughters Kaitlin and Kelsey are living. It is now 2003, and Andrew has had two more children — Kerry and Kyle — but no grandchildren.

52.   What interest does Kerry own in the land?

   (A)   Vested remainder for life.

   (B)   Contingent remainder for life. *mascertainelle*

   (C)   Shifting executory interest for life.

   (D)   None.

The Midwestern Automotive Society conveys a former used car lot "to Alexandra for life, then to Alexandra's siblings." Alexandra's parents are alive, and Alexandra has a brother Bertrand and a sister Sonja.

53.   Is Bertrand's property interest valid under the traditional common law Rule against Perpetuities?

   (A)   Yes, because it is not subject to the Rule.

   (B)   Yes, using Alexandra as the measuring life.

   (C)   Yes, using Alexandra's parents as the measuring life.

   (D)   No, because Alexandra's parents might have more children.

William Henderson Johnson III just died with a will leaving "all of my earthly belongings to Stuart for life, remainder to such of Stuart's lineal descendants as are alive on January 1, 2010."

54.   Who *cannot* serve as the measuring life to validate the contingent remainder held by "such of Stuart's lineal descendants as are alive on January 1, 2010"?

   (A)   Stuart.

   (B)   Stuart's current wife.

   (C)   Any of Stuart's living children.

(D) Any of Stuart's children who are born after William died but before January 1, 2010.

In 2000, the Acme Steel Company sells the site of a defunct factory "to Andrew for life, remainder to Beatrice." Ten months later, Andrew sells his interest to Cooper. Alas, Cooper dies of a mysterious illness in December 2002. Andrew and Beatrice are both alive.

55. Who owns the present possessory interest in the land?

   (A) Cooper's heirs.

   (B) Andrew.

   (C) Beatrice.

   (D) The Acme Steel Company.

Angela was born in 1936. She never married, and she does not have any children. She does own lots of land, though. So in 1990, Angela wrote a will devising all of her land "to my favorite nephew Jackson for life, then to the first daughter of Jackson whenever born who becomes a medical doctor." Jackson's first daughter Jenny is born in 1999, a few months before Angela dies. Jackson has not had any more daughters since then, and Jenny is in grade school.

56. Jenny owns what interest in the land?

   (A) None.

   (B) Vested remainder.

   (C) Contingent remainder.

   (D) Shifting executory interest.

57. Which of the following is *not* an accurate description of the concept of a fee tail?

   (A) A fee tail facilitated the alienability of property.

   (B) A fee tail could be created by a conveyance "to Charlotte and the heirs of her body."

   (C) A fee tail was designed to keep land within the same family for several generations.

   (D) A life estate is the modern device most likely to replace the functioning of a fee tail.

Luke Paulsen began his working career selling groceries, but he now sees an unprecedented business opportunity in sporting goods. He plans to operate Luke's Sporting Goods, a store that sells a variety of equipment for a variety of sporting endeavors.

58. If he does so, he will hold the title in fee simple absolute to which of the following properties?

   (A) Orangeacre, which was conveyed from Lauer's Real Estate "to Luke so long as the land is used for a grocery store."

(B)   Blueacre, which was conveyed from Luke "to Lauer's Real Estate <u>with the understanding</u> that the land will belong to Luke if he needs it for a sporting goods store."   *not legally operative*

(C)   Greenacre, which was conveyed from Lauer's Real Estate "to Luke provided that he uses the land for a grocery store, but if the land is not used as a grocery store, then to Luke's son Tom."

(D)   Yellowacre, which Luke once owned in fee simple, and then conveyed "to Lauer's Real Estate while I operate my grocery store there." Lauer's Real Estate then conveyed a life estate "to Luke so long as he sells tennis balls on the property."

Joyce and Cathy were law school roommates in the 1970's, and they have remained best friends. They are both 55 years old. Cathy has two sons, while Joyce does not have any children.

59.   Joyce owns a shifting executory interest in which of the following properties?

(A)   A lake house that Cathy conveyed in 2000 "to Joyce until her sons graduate from college."

(B)   A ranch that Cathy conveyed in 2003 "to the Western Historical Society for the rest of my life, then to Joyce."

(C)   Ten acres of forested land that Cathy conveyed in 1994 "to the city so long as the land is open to the public for recreational purposes for the next 20 years, then to Joyce."

(D)   A vacant suburban lot that Cathy's <u>will</u> devises "to the West Park Synagogue provided that it is used for religious <u>purposes</u> for the next 20 years, then to Joyce."   *not yet legally operative*

In February 2000, the Axle Motor Company conveyed its riverfront property "to Lucy Brewer for life, then to her eldest daughter." At the time of the conveyance, Lucy has two daughters: Annie, age 16; and Tanya, age 12. Two years later, when she turned 18, Annie conveyed her interest in the land to the Prairie Land Trust. At the same time, Lucy leased the property "to Dean Walter for five years." In January 2003, Lucy and Annie die in a car accident.

60.   Who is most likely to have the possessory interest in the land following the fatal accident?

le

not e d then living

(A)   The Axle Motor Company.

(B)   The Prairie Land Trust.

(C)   Tanya.

(D)   Dean Walter.

Jane McCartney has given land to each of her children when they got married. Her youngest daughter Julie is not married, but she has been living with Henry for five years, and they have two children together. So, in 2001, Jane conveyed ten acres "to Julie and Henry as tenants by the entirety, but if they ever get divorced, then to Julie." In 2003, Julie and Henry got married.

61. Upon her marriage, one of the interests that Julie owns in the land is:

    (A) A tenancy by the entirety.

    (B) A joint tenancy or a tenancy in common, depending upon the jurisdiction.

    (C) A contingent remainder.

    (D) A springing executory interest.

The Mountain Realty Company conveyed ten acres of land "to Elaine for life." Two years later, Elaine drafted a will devising all of her property to her son Randy. Then Randy sold his interest in the land "to Sara so long as she does not allow a SUV to enter the property." Next Elaine sold the land "to the county for use as a park." Finally, Elaine dies.

62. Who owns the possessory interest in the ten acres of land?

    (A) Mountain Realty Company.

    (B) Randy.

    (C) Sara.

    (D) The county.

In 2001, Gerald died with a will that devised his home "to my eldest daughter Carla for her home, then to Carla's children." When Gerald died, Carla was a single mother of twin baby boys Thomas and Mark.

63. What property interest is Mark most likely to have in the home?

    (A) A vested remainder subject to opening.

    (B) A contingent remainder subject to opening.

    (C) A shifting executory interest.

    (D) None.

Donald Ferguson began fishing for salmon in New Campbell in 1985. He married Beth Ferguson in 1991. The fishery in the region became depleted, so in 1993 the federal government established an individual fishing quota (IFQ) program that limited the annual number of salmon that any person could take to 1,000 fish per year that the person has been fishing there. The right to take 1,000 fish is worth about $100,000, so by 2003 Donald's IFQ was worth $1,800,000. Donald and Beth are getting divorced, and Beth believes that she is entitled to her share of the IFQ.

64. At the time of their divorce in 2003, what rights — if any — does Beth have in the rights established by the IFQ?

ANSWER:

Shortly after they were married, George and Sylvia purchased a house in New Campbell as tenants by the entirety. Ten years later, they agreed to live apart for a while to see if they could work out their differences. Sylvia continued to live in the house. Before George moved out, Sylvia told him that they should sell the house and divide the proceeds equally if they could not reconcile their marriage. Sylvia dies in a car accident five weeks after George moves out. Her will devises all of her property to her sister Betsy.

65. Who owns what interest in the house?

ANSWER:

In 1955, three brothers — Alex, Bobby, and Carlos — purchased ten acres of land as joint tenants. Four years later, Alex got married, and he conveyed all of his property to his new wife Doris. Next, in 1970, Bobby died, devising all of his property to his three children, Eduardo, Francesco, and Gloria. Finally, in 2002, Carlos and then Eduardo died, with Eduardo's wife Henrietta inheriting all of his property and with Carlos devising his interest in the ten acres of land to Gloria, his favorite niece.

66. Who owns what interest in the ten acres of land?

ANSWER:

Melinda and Brandon are getting a divorce after twelve years of marriage. They have two significant assets: a mutual fund which contains the income that Brandon earned and which is now worth $300,000, and a $60,000 car that was a gift to Brandon from his parents five years ago.

67. In a community property state, Melinda is most likely entitled to:

(A) An equitable distribution of the mutual fund and value of the car.

(B) Neither the car nor the mutual fund.

(C) $180,000.

(D) An equal distribution of the mutual fund.

In 1990, Alice and Gerald were married. Ten years later, they purchased a vacation home as tenants by the entirety. Then, Gerald lost his lucrative job managing a global mutual fund when the stock market lost much of its value. Gerald was desperate to fend off his creditors, so he sold them his interest in the vacation home. One month later, Gerald dies, devising all of his property to his children.

68. What interest do Gerald's creditors have in the vacation home?

(A) They own it in fee simple.

(B) They own it as tenants in common with Alice.

(C) They own it as tenants in common with Alice and with Gerald's children.

(D) They do not have any interest in it.

Frank and Joseph lived together as a gay couple in a house they bought as tenants in common. Ten months ago, their relationship ended, and Frank moved out of the house. Frank has since conveyed his interest in the house to Kelly, who is a local real estate agent. Kelly wants to sell the house, but Joseph would rather keep it.

69. Kelly will:

(A) Be able to sell the house because an out-of-possession owner has superior rights to the possessing owner.

(B) Be able to sell the house as the result of a partition action.

(C) Not be able to sell the house because Joseph obtained the fee simple title to the house when Frank tried to sell it.

(D) Not be able to sell the house if Joseph pays Kelly rent for living there.

Harry and Winona own a beachside home as joint tenants.

70. Which of the following actions is most likely to destroy their joint tenancy?

(A) They decide to separate.

(B) They have children.

(C) Winona takes out a mortgage on the house.

(D) Harry sells his interest in the house to his parents.

71. The traditional common law doctrine of dower provided wives whose husbands had died with the functional equivalent of:

(A) A fee simple.

(B) A fee simple determinable.

(C) A life estate.

(D) No property rights.

Eric and Anita have been married since 1987.

72. Which of the following is most likely to be treated as property owned by both Eric and Anita if they got divorced?

(A) The law degree that Eric earned in 1986.

(B) Eric's income as the partner in a law firm.

(C) The contingency fee agreements that Eric has with several clients who are plaintiffs in multi-million dollar tort lawsuits.

(D) The yacht that Eric received in 2001 as a fortieth birthday present from his parents.

John and Jim own their lakeside cottage as co-tenants.

73. Jim must obtain John's consent before Jim can take which action?

(A) Invite the police to search the cottage's kitchen when they knock on the door and ask for such permission.

(B) Tear down the cottage and replace it with a larger home.

(C) Obtain a mortgage from the local bank for the cottage.

(D) Sell his interest to a couple who hopes to retire in the cottage someday.

Anita and Greg were married in Texas in 1990, and they have lived there ever since then. Greg drove a pickup truck that the couple bought in 2000, while Anita drove an old sports car. The couple separated in the summer of 2001. Shortly thereafter, Anita went to visit Greg at his new home. Greg was sitting in his pickup truck in his driveway, and Anita parked behind him, blocking him. Anita tried to "talk" to Greg, but he remained in his locked vehicle. When Greg would not roll his window down, Anita returned to her car and grabbed her keys. She then used the keys to severely scratch the paint on the passenger side and tailgate of Greg's truck. Subsequently, Greg sued Anita for damaging his property.

74. Greg's lawsuit will:

(A) Succeed, because Anita had no property interest in the pickup truck.

(B) Succeed, because Anita's actions constituted waste.

(C)   Fail, if Anita held the title to the truck.

(D)   Fail, because Anita had the right to damage their truck.

Alma owned a twenty acre farm. In 2000, her nephew Sebastian married Cheryl. One year later, Sebastian purchased ten acres of Alma's farm. Then, in 2002, Cheryl purchased the other ten acres of Alma's farm.

75.   As a result of these transactions, Sebastian and Cheryl own:

(A)   The twenty acres as tenants by the entirety.

(B)   The twenty acres as joint tenants.

(C)   The twenty acres as tenants in common.

(D)   The two ten acre parcels separately.

76. What are the advantages and disadvantages of relying upon the Civil Rights Act of 1866 (codified at 42 U.S.C. § 1982) instead of the Fair Housing Act in housing discrimination cases?

ANSWER: adv not subject to single family exception nor 4 dwelling exception

In 1968, the District of Columbia Court of Appeals held that a lease for an apartment whose condition violates the housing code is void. Since then, no other jurisdiction has adopted that rule.

77. Why has the illegal lease doctrine failed to gain popularity as a means of responding to concerns about adequate housing?

ANSWER: iwh already addresses

Terri Tenant rents an apartment from Lou Landlord. Two months after Terri moves into the apartment with her two toddlers, she learns that the residents in the apartment next door sell crack cocaine to children in the neighborhood. Terri tells Lou, but he does nothing.

78. What actions can Terri take in response?

ANSWER: constructive eviction – breach of K quiet enjoyment
stop rent – iwh

Many academics question the effectiveness of rent controls in assuring affordable housing, yet such controls persist in some jurisdictions.

79. What are the arguments advanced by supporters of rent controls?

ANSWER: keep housing affordable for low class

Alabama is one of the few states that fails to recognize an implied warranty of habitability. The state's supreme court has explained that "while we could recognize an implied warranty of habitability, as the tenant requests, we are of the opinion that the best forum for making a change in our law is the legislature."

80. What is the best response that justifies judicial establishment of such an implied warranty?

ANSWER: *public policy, safety*

81. Which rent control ordinance is most likely to be held unconstitutional?

    (A) An ordinance that omits a declaration that it is responding to a wartime emergency.

    (B) An ordinance that determines the permissible rent that a landlord may charge by calculating the sum of the landlord's operating expenses and debt service and then ensuring that the landlord receives gross rents greater than that amount.

    (C) An ordinance that determines the permissible rent that a landlord may charge by authorizing the landlord to raise rents at one-half the annual rate of inflation.

    (D) An ordinance that allows the children of a tenant to remain in the apartment at the same rent once the tenant dies.

Tori and Janice Paul rent a home to Reginald Carter.

82. The Pauls will not be liable for breaching an implied warranty of habitability if:

    (A) Carter signed a written waiver of the warranty when he agreed to lease the apartment.

    (B) The problems about which Carter complains did not exist at the time that his lease commenced.

    (C) They tried but failed to fix the problems about which Carter complained.

    (D) Carter rented a retail store from them.

The Utah Mobile Home Park Residency Act prohibits the owner of a mobile home park from terminating a resident's lease without cause.

83. The statute thus modifies which common law tenancy?

    (A) Term of years.

    (B) Periodic tenancy.

    (C) Both term of years and periodic tenancy.

    (D) Neither term of years nor periodic tenancy. *at will*

On March 20, 1998, Jackson signed a lease to rent Dave's vacation home in southern Virginia for the two year period from June 1, 1998, to May 31, 2000. Eager to enjoy the home, Jackson drove across the country with his family to begin their vacation. But when they arrived on June 4, 1998, the house was occupied by four different individuals.

84. According to the American rule, Dave has breached an implied covenant with respect to each of the following individuals found at the house *except*:

(A) Dave himself, who decided he really liked the house.

(B) Dave's son Kyle, who received his dad's permission to use the house for a fishing trip.

(C) Bob Clauss, who produces a deed indicating that he owns the house, and Dave does not own the house.

(D) John Crosby, who grew up in the neighborhood and always wanted to spend some time in the house.

85. Which tenant is most likely to be able to leave her premises without having to pay further rent or otherwise honor the terms of the lease?

(A) Despite Linus Landlord's repeated repair attempts, the water in Tanya Tenant's apartment has not worked since she moved in six weeks ago.

(B) The air conditioning in Terri Tenant's apartment breaks down on an afternoon when it is 104 degrees outside, and Lou Landlord tells her that he will not be able to fix it until the next day.

(C) Twyla Tenant suspects that the two men who live in the apartment unit next to her are dealing drugs.

(D) The lock on the front door of Tori Tenant's store has not worked since she rented the premises thirteen months ago, but Larry Landlord tells her that she should fix it herself.

Rachel enters into a lease with Apartments, Inc., to rent an apartment. The lease signed by the parties provides that it may be terminated by either party "upon zero days notice."

86. The most likely characterization of the lease is that it creates:

(A) An estate of years.

(B) A periodic estate.

(C) An estate at will.

(D) An estate at sufferance.

Roberto owns two acres of land on the outskirts of Chicago that he leased to Julia for ten years beginning on April 21, 1998. It is now December 15, 1999.

87. Which of the following agreements is most likely to be judged a partial assignment?

(A) Julia rents the two acres to Franklin for the period from December 15, 1999, to April 21, 2008.

(B) Julia rents one acre to Franklin for the period from December 15, 1999, to April 21, 2008.

(C) Julia rents two acres to Franklin for the period from December 15, 1999, to April 21, 2006.

(D)   Julia rents one acre to Franklin for the period from December 15, 1999, to April 21, 2006.

Susan does not want to ever speak to her landlord Isaac again. She wants to know whether she will be able to move out of her apartment without informing Isaac that she is leaving or without Isaac informing her that she wants to end the lease, no matter how long she has to wait.

88.   She will be able to do so if she has:

(A)   A term of years.

(B)   A periodic tenancy.

(C)   A tenancy at will.

(D)   Any of the above.

In January 1995, Lance Landlord leased his country estate to Thelma Tenant for ten years at a monthly rent of $10,000. Thelma immediately moved into the estate. Then in August 2000, while Thelma was out of the country on a weekend trip, Francis Freeloader moved into the estate and installed her bodyguards to prevent anyone — including Thelma — from entering the property. It took Thelma four months to get the local government to evict Francis so that Thelma could move back into the estate in December 2000. Thelma refuses to pay Lance any rent for the four months that Francis possessed the house.

89.   Which resulting lawsuit is most likely to be successful?

(A)   Lance's suit against Thelma for the $40,000 unpaid rent.

(B)   Lance's suit against Francis for the $40,000 unpaid rent.

(C)   Thelma's suit against Lance for breach of an implied covenant if the American rule applies.

(D)   Thelma's suit against Lance for breach of an implied covenant if the English rule applies.

90.   Which landlord is most likely to be liable to the tenant?

(A)   Lois Landlord obtains a court order, evicts Tom Tenant while he is taking an exam, and leaves Tenant's belongings outside in the rain.

(B)   Lou Landlord worries that Thelma Tenant is destroying his office building, so he changes the locks on the building on a Sunday morning.

(C)   Larry Landlord dislikes the kinds of friends who visit Teresa Tenant at her apartment, so he refuses to renew her lease once it expires.

(D)   Lily Landlord refuses to allow Tim Tenant to install a special telephone line that Tenant had requested and volunteered to pay for himself because he is deaf.

91.   Which of the following landlords is least likely to be able to terminate his lease with the tenant as the landlord desires to do so?

(A) In 1997, Teresa Tenant entered into a five-year lease with Larry Landlord. Larry now wants to terminate the lease, so he called Teresa on the phone, and she agreed to terminate the lease and move out at the end of the month.

(B) In 1995, Twyla Tenant entered into a four-year lease with Louis Landlord. After four years, Twyla wanted to stay on the premises, but Louis refused to let her do so.

(C) In 1996, Tanya Tenant entered into a _tenancy at will_ with Lars Landlord. Two years later, Lars asked Tanya to leave the premises by the end of the next day, but she refused.

(D) In 1998, Tori Tenant entered into a _periodic tenancy_ with Lyle Landlord. Two years later, Lyle asked Tori to leave the premises by the end of the next day, but she refused.

In August 1999, Sonja Student rented an apartment near campus for $200 per month for a one year term. In February 2000, Sonja wrote her landlord a note stating that "I am leaving this dump because the lock on the front door never works, and I'm not going to pay you another dime."

92. She will be able to abandon the premises and stop paying rent even though:

(A) The apartment is located in a rural area of South Coleman where no one ever locks their doors.

(B) Sonja never told the landlord that the lock did not work.

(C) The lease stated that Sonja waived any warranties of habitability.

(D) Sonja replaced the original door with one of her own choosing.

93. Housing codes have been criticized for failing to provide an adequate supply of good housing because:

(A) They are too vague.

(B) Few jurisdictions have enacted them.

(C) Courts have resisted legislative intrusions into the determination of the relative rights of landlords and tenants.

(D) They do not provide landlords with an adequate incentive to maintain their buildings.

Tom Tenant wants to rent an apartment from Louise Landlord. Landlord does not want to rent the apartment to Tenant, but she wants to comply with the Fair Housing Act.

94. From the perspective of the FHA, the worst reason that Louise can offer for refusing to rent the apartment to Tom is that he is:

(A) Gay.

(B) The father of six children.

    (C)   A troublemaker.

    (D)   A law student.

The Restaurant Association of America (RAA) has rented property from the Urban Realty Partnership (URP).

  95.   In which instance is the RAA still obligated to pay rent to URP?

    (A)°   The RAA entered into a tenancy at will with URP for a downtown lot on which the RAA planned to host an outdoor demonstration kitchen, but which the RAA decided it could not afford to operate given an economic downturn.

    (B)   The RAA rented an office suite in a building owned by URP which the city condemned by its eminent domain power, tore down, and replaced it with a new sports stadium.

    (C)°   The RAA entered into a five year lease with URP for three floors in a downtown office tower, then three months later the RAA leased those three floors for three years to a local law firm that offered to pay the RAA double the rental amount to use those three floors for the next three years. Within the year, the law firm disbanded and stopped paying rent to the RAA.

    (D)   The RAA rented a convention center from URP in order to host its annual convention, but it had to cancel the convention because of the sudden outbreak of a deadly epidemic in the city two weeks before the event was scheduled to occur.

Doctor Suarez owned a house in the town of University Park. Suarez was engaged in an experimental medical practice hundreds of miles away, so he wanted to make sure that the house was occupied while he was living outside of town. Money was not a problem for Suarez, so he did not need to charge rent. Accordingly, Suarez rented the house to Sandy and Greg, who were students attending the medical school in University Park. The lease provided, in total, that "the tenants [Sandy and Greg] are hereby allowed to live in the house until one month after the owner [Dr. Suarez] notifies the tenants that he is returning to live there himself." Six months later, Sandy and Greg informed Suarez that they planned to move to a different house that was closer to campus.   *p +*

  96.   Suarez's lawsuit against Sandy and Greg will:

    (A)   Succeed if Suarez demands that Sandy and Greg pay the fair rental value of the property.

    (B)   Succeed if Suarez demands that Sandy and Greg live in the house until Suarez returns to town.

    (C)°   Fail because the lease did not identify the remedy that would be available to Suarez if Sandy and Greg breached their obligations.

    (D)   Fail because Sandy and Greg provided adequate notice that they were leaving.

Each year Lois Landlord rents out her extra bedroom to two college students. Tom and Doris want to rent that bedroom, but Lois refuses because she has a religious objection to unmarried students of the opposite sex living together.

97.   The legality of Lois's decision is most likely to be determined by:

   (A)   The constitutionality of the federal Religious Land Use and Institutionalized Person Act.

   (B)   The interpretation of the federal Fair Housing Act.

   (C)   The scope of state or local civil rights laws.

   (D)   The common law rule adopted by the jurisdiction.

In 1996, Stella sold ten acres of land in New Campbell to Justin for $100,000. Justin did not record the conveyance, and he never actually set foot on the property. In 1997, Stella gave the same ten acres to Quincy as a present for his 21st birthday. Quincy did not know about the earlier conveyance to Justin, and he immediately recorded the conveyance. Justin and Quincy now dispute ownership of the property.

98. Who owns the property?

ANSWER:

In 1962, the Jacksons and the Madisons purchased adjoining property along the White River. Over the next 15 years, the course of the river moved 20 feet to the east, leaving additional land next to both the original properties owned by the Jacksons and the Madisons. During that same time, the Jacksons managed a family farm on their land and on all of the land created by the shifting of the river, while the Madisons lived in Chicago, hoping to retire along their White River land one day. In 1990, when the Madisons returned to their land for the first time since 1962, they discovered that the Jacksons had fenced all of the riverfront land as pasture for their grazing cattle. The Madisons ordered the Jacksons to get off of their land, but the Jacksons insisted that the land was actually theirs.

99. Who owns the new land between the Madisons' 1962 boundary and the river today?

ANSWER:

During a romantic candlelight dinner conversation in December 1987, Jim Welchans agreed to sell Dawn Donatelli his country estate in South Coleman for $300,000. One day later, Jackson McCartney — the attorney for both Jim and Dawn — prepared a deed for the conveyance, which Jim then signed and gave back to Jackson to give to Dawn. But before Jackson could give the deed to her, Dawn called to indicate that she was having second thoughts about the deal. Jim and Dawn never talked about the conveyance again. In 1994, Jim sold the property to Madison, who converted the estate into a bed and breakfast that now earns millions of dollars annually. Then, in 1998, Dawn walked onto the property carrying the deed that Jim had signed in 1987. Dawn explained that she got the deed from Jackson the day before in a pile of old files that he returned to her because she had hired a new attorney.

100. Who owns the property?

ANSWER:

101. Why are commercial airliners able to fly across land owned by thousands of individuals without committing a trespass?

ANSWER:

A 1904 compact between the States of Oregon and Washington provided that Wanapam Island, then a modest three acres, was part of Oregon despite its location on Washington's side of the common boundary of the states. After 1927, when the United States decided to use the island for a Coast Guard station, the national government began placing fill around its shoreline and over the next 42 years added some 24.5 acres to the area of the original island.

102. Is Oregon or Washington the sovereign authority over this filled land?

ANSWER:

103. Which party is most likely able to keep the most of the goods that she made?

(A) Anna, who watched a meteor fall from the sky onto her neighbor's backyard, ran over and took it, and used the stone to make several dozen inexpensive necklaces.

(B) Betty, who snuck into her neighbor's stream, panned for gold, melted the gold dust that she found, and crafted a small ring.

(C) Celia, who accidentally mixed the grapes that she harvested from her vineyard with grapes that she accidentally harvested from her neighbor's land, and then produced an award-winning wine.

(D) Daphne, who got lost in the woods behind her house and accidentally wandered onto her neighbor's land, found an empty turtle shell, brought it home and painted it blue, and gave it to her six-year-old daughter to play with as a toy.

104. A landowner is most likely to be able to take exclusive possession of all of which resource that lies beneath both her land and the land of her neighbor?

(A) Groundwater.

(B) Natural gas.

(C) A cave.

(D) Native American relics.

Arthur and Evalyn Koester had one child, their son Randall. On February 14, 1974, a developer conveyed a vacant residential lot in South Coleman "to Arthur and/or Randall Koester." In 1982, Arthur and Evalyn built their retirement home on the lot. Arthur died in 1983, devising all of his property to Evalyn. In May 1983, Evalyn moved into the newly constructed home.

She has lived there ever since, and she has paid the property taxes, built a second-floor addition, and rented out part of the home. Randall has never lived there, nor has he paid any of the taxes or shared in any of the rent. It was not until 1995 that Evalyn discovered that Randall was listed on the original 1974 conveyance of the lot. When Evalyn mentioned this to Randall, he angrily promised to assert his legal rights to the property.

105. What interests do Evalyn and Randall have in the property?

(A) Evalyn and Randall own the land as joint tenants.

(B) Evalyn and Randall own the land as tenants in common.

(C) Randall owns the lot in fee simple, and Evalyn owns nothing.

(D) Evalyn owns the lot in fee simple, and Randall owns nothing.

106. One of the justifications for obtaining title to land by adverse possession is:

(A) Land is more important than personal property.

(B) Those who knowingly trespass upon land that is not being used should be rewarded.

(C) No recording system is capable of determining who really owns the land.

(D) The policies supporting statutes of limitations are applicable to landowners.

107. Which of the following actions is most likely to be held to be a trespass of Julia's property?

(A) Her neighbor's pet dog wandered on to Julia's land to fetch a stick.

(B) Tiny particulates that cannot be seen by the naked eye float through the air across Julia's land.

(C) The lights from the local park shine onto Julia's land during summer nights when softball games are played.

(D) The police cut across Julia's land to head off a fleeing bank robber.

In 1976, Albert conveyed a parcel of land to Cheryl pursuant to a deed stating that Albert "hereby covenants and warrants to Cheryl that he owns title to the land free of all liens and encumbrances." Shortly thereafter, Cheryl conveyed the land to Dennis pursuant to a deed providing that "Cheryl does hereby grant, bargain, and convey her interest in the land to Dennis." Dennis then obtained a mortgage on the land from the St. Paul Bank. Unfortunately for Dennis, he soon defaulted on the mortgage. Unfortunately for the bank, it was then learned that Albert never owned the land, so Dennis did not own it when he obtained the mortgage.

108. St. Paul will be able to recover damages based on the liability of:

(A) Albert and Cheryl.

(B) Albert, but not Cheryl.

(C) Cheryl, but not Albert.

(D)   Neither Albert nor Cheryl.

109.   Which of the following is *not* a possible remedy for a trespass onto someone's land?

(A)   Imprisonment.

(B)   Monetary damages.

(C)   Ejectment.

(D)   Forfeiture.

After election day on November 7, 2000, Lisa Whittemore placed a "Bush for President" sign in her front yard. Soon thereafter, Lisa received a letter from her homeowner's association informing her that a covenant attached to her property prohibits political signs except during the month *before* election day.

110.   What is Lisa's best legal authority for her ability to keep her sign in her front yard?

ANSWER:

You own a house in the Eagle Nest residential development. It is your vacation house and you spend about six long weekends a year there; the rest of the time you rent the house to others. The Eagle Nest Homeowner's Association has just increased the monthly parking fee for nonresident owners (like you) to $75 per month. Resident owners still pay the old fee of $25 per month. When you ask the homeowner's association why it adopted the new fee, it explains that it wants to prevent nonresident owners from realizing a profit by renting out their parking spaces to tenants at market rates.

111.   Is the homeowner's association's $75 per month parking fee for nonresidents valid?

ANSWER:

The Blue River runs through a series of striking landscapes. Fearing the developing of the land, in 1992 the Blue River Conservation Coalition (BRCC) acquired a conservation easement from Patricia Campbell, the owner of the land adjoining a 30-mile stretch of the river. The easement prohibited Campbell from "taking or authorizing any actions that would destroy the wildlife habitat, ecosystems, and natural beauty of the land." Then, in 2000, Campbell conveyed her fee simple interest in the same land to BRCC except that Campbell retained a life estate subject to the easement in the land. But BRCC soon faced financial pressures, and in August 2001 it sold the land to Dave Johansen, a local developer. Campbell died three months later.

112.   Does the easement continue to restrict Johansen's activities on the land?

ANSWER:

During the middle of the twentieth century, numerous courts confronted claims alleging that the presence of a cemetery in a residential area constituted a private nuisance because the constant reminder of death interfered with the ability of neighbors to enjoy their property. Most of those claims failed.

113. Why does the presence of a cemetery not constitute a private nuisance?

ANSWER:

In 1989, the Glen Theater Corporation entered into a 10-year lease on a building owned by Acme Realty. The lease required Glen Theater to pay a security deposit of $22,500. The lease further stated that "(1) the landlord shall return the security deposit to the tenant if the tenant pays all of the rent owed under the lease, (2) the landlord is not responsible for any repairs or maintenance of the building, and (3) all of the covenants in the lease run with the land." In 1993, Acme sold the building to Growth Realty. After the lease expired in 1999, Glen Theater asked Growth to return the security deposit, but Growth refused.

114. Will Glen Theater succeed in its lawsuit against Growth to recover the security deposit?

ANSWER:

115. An easement by necessity exists whenever:

(A) Someone has walked across a path on their neighbor's land for twenty years.

(B) The closest path from your property to the highway is across your neighbor's land.

(C) Your neighbor enters into a written agreement with you that allows you to cross her land to get to the highway because otherwise it would be extremely difficult for you to do so.

(D) You buy land from your neighbor and the only path to the highway is across the rest of your neighbor's property.

116. A landowner who conveys a conservation easement:

(A) Must be paid the fair market value of the property.

(B) Should experience reduced tax payments.

(C) Can no longer use the property subject to the easement.

(D) Cannot sell the property without the consent of the easement holder.

117. The absence of horizontal privity might prevent Peter from winning which of the following lawsuits?

(A) After they had lived next to each other for five years, Peter and Elizabeth signed an agreement promising to always paint their houses the same shade of blue.

Shortly thereafter, Elizabeth sold her property to Grace. Grace then began to paint her house red. Peter has sued Grace to recover $3,000 as compensation for the injuries that the sight of the different paint caused him.

(B) Elizabeth owned two neighboring lots. When she sold one of the lots to Peter, they signed an agreement promising to always paint their houses the same shade of blue. Shortly thereafter, Elizabeth sold her property to Grace. Grace then began to paint her house red. Peter has sued Grace to recover $3,000 as compensation for the injuries that the sight of the different paint caused him.

(C) After they had lived next to each other for five years, Peter and Elizabeth signed an agreement promising to always paint their houses the same shade of blue. Shortly thereafter, Elizabeth sold her property to Grace. Grace then began to paint her house red. Peter has sued Grace to enjoin her from painting her house red.

(D) Elizabeth owned two neighboring lots. When she sold one of the lots to Peter, they signed an agreement promising to always paint their houses the same shade of blue. Shortly thereafter, Elizabeth sold her property to Grace. Grace then began to paint her house red. Peter has sued Grace to enjoin her from painting her house red.

In 1976, Nancy Clay purchased a house in a new subdivision. Because the lot was on the side of a hill, she terraced her backyard to divert rainfall away from the house to prevent flooding and stop erosion. The lot behind her house was vacant until 1998, when Jim Lake purchased the lot from the developer and built a house there. Jim built an exotic Japanese garden behind his house, unknowingly extending half of the garden onto Nancy's terraced backyard. But Jim was transferred to another city soon after finishing the garden, so in July 1999 he sold his property to Peggy Kiser, who chose the house because of her love for Japanese gardens. One month later, Nancy asked Peggy to remove the half of the garden that was on Nancy's property. Peggy really wants to be able to keep the garden intact.

118. It is most likely that she has:

(A) A prescriptive easement.

(B) An easement by necessity.

(C) An easement by estoppel.

(D) No right to use Nancy's land.

John owns a large estate that has been in his family for several generations, but he cannot afford to maintain it. Accordingly, in 1992 John conveyed Blueacre to Jim with a covenant that prohibited the use of the land for a dog kennel. Three years later, John conveyed Greenacre to Susan without any covenants. Finally, in 2000, John conveyed Yellowacre to Lisa with a covenant the prohibited the use of the land for a dog kennel. Blueacre, Greenacre, and Yellowacre are adjacent properties in what used to constitute John's family estate.

119. Which of the following parties is least likely to be able to enforce the covenant as they desire?

(A) Lisa wants to enforce the covenant against Susan.

(B) Susan wants to enforce the covenant against Lisa.

(C) Susan wants to enforce the covenant against Jim.

(D) Lisa wants to enforce the covenant against Jim.

120. According to the terminology of Professors Calabresi and Malamed, state statutes that prevent farming operations from being challenged as nuisances are examples of:

(A) A plaintiff protected by a property rule.

(B) A plaintiff protected by a liability rule.

(C) A defendant protected by a property rule.

(D) A defendant protected by a liability rule.

In 1990, Donna Developer transformed her family's historic estate into Plantation Acres, a subdivision containing 200 single-family homes. Three years later, Cathy Carlson bought one of the homes in the subdivision. Cathy enjoys the peaceful atmosphere of the neighborhood so much that several of her colleagues have bought homes there, too. In 1998, however, Cathy was distressed to see that one of her colleagues who had just moved in next door, Sandy Skelly, was building an addition on to the front of his house to store the antique gasoline pumps that he sells over the Internet.

121. Cathy is most likely able to stop Sandy from building the addition if:

(A) The family who owned the house before Sandy purchased it used the property only for residential purposes.

(B) Cathy bought the house because the prior owner assured her that only residential homes could be built in the area.

(C) A survey of a majority of the homeowners in Plantation Acres shows that they oppose the operation of a business out of a home in the subdivision.

(D) Most of the lots originally created by Donna contained covenants that the property could only be used for residential purposes.

Nancy Neighbor lives in an older suburb where the houses are located close to one another. She has built six-foot-high concrete walls along both sides of her property. She built the wall to separate her house from Billy Ball's property because she wanted to prevent the Ball children from playing in her yard. She built the other wall separating her house from Andy Annoying simply because she hated Andy and knew that he hated concrete walls.

122. Which factor best explains why a court will enjoin the wall separating Nancy's property from Andy as a nuisance, but not the wall separating Nancy's property from Billy?

(A) The nuisance per se doctrine.

(B)   The gravity of the harm.

(C)   The utility of the conduct.

(D)   The coming to the nuisance doctrine.

123.   Which of the following agreements is most likely to be enforceable against Kim?

(A)   In 1992, George bought a house for $200,000, paying $40,000 in cash and securing a $160,000 mortgage from Third Bank. In 1999, Kim bought the house from George for $220,000 in cash. George took the money and immediately flew to Belize. Third Bank now wants Kim to pay the balance of George's mortgage.

(B)   Kim and Herb own neighboring ranches in Colorado. In 1981, they entered into a written agreement that allocated the right to use the water from a small lake that bordered their ranches. The agreement also stated that if it was ever necessary for a court to adjudicate their water rights under the agreement, then the prevailing party was entitled to attorney's fees. In 1999, Kim and Herb litigated a dispute about their rights under the agreement, and when Herb prevailed, he sought attorney's fees from Kim.

(C)   In 1990, Kara purchased two acres in the Wooded Canyon subdivision. She built a house on the western half of her property, and in 1993, she sold the eastern half of the land to Kim. As part of the agreement, Kim and Kara promised each other that they would babysit each other's children once a week. Kim then took a job that required her to travel on business for weeks at a time, and Kara is now seeking to enforce the babysitting agreement.

(D)   In 1998, Kim purchased a half-acre lot from Susan with the agreement that Kim would build a Colonial style house on the property. Shortly thereafter, Kim met Aaron Architect, who sketched the plans for a spacious home that would look like a Swiss chalet. Kim wants to build a home based on Aaron's plans, but Susan objects.

124.   If you are trying to persuade a state that horizontal privity should no longer be a requirement for a real covenant to be enforceable, the *least* persuasive argument is that:

(A)   Horizontal privity is duplicative of vertical privity.

(B)   Many jurisdictions have already dropped the requirement of horizontal privity.

(C)   The reasons for requiring horizontal privity are primarily historical.

(D)   Other tests can better determine whether or not a covenant should be enforceable.

In 1966, Adam and Eve built houses on adjacent properties. Since the only road to Eve's house was across Adam's land, Eve paid $2,000 for "the right to use the road to gain access to and from" her house.

125.   Eve would retain that right even if:

(A) Eve repeatedly drove on other parts of Adam's land despite his protests.

(B) Adam blocked the road in 1976 and Eve never complained.

(C) The construction of a new highway enabled Eve to reach her property without crossing Adam's land.

(D) Eve bought Adam's land.

Rob and Jerry have owned neighboring houses in New Rochelle since 1962. Soon after they purchased their properties, they discovered that the lengthy circular driveway that runs between their houses was in fact located entirely on Rob's property. Jerry then purchased an easement from Rob "to use the driveway for ingress and egress to Jerry's property." Over the years, Jerry planted two dozen cherry trees alongside the part of the driveway nearest his house. The trees were on the part of Rob's property across which Jerry had an easement. But after Rob moved and sold his property to Lou in 1998, Lou took out his chain saw and prepared to cut down the cherry trees.

126. Jerry's suit to block Lou from cutting the trees will:

(A) Succeed because Jerry has an express easement that gives him the right to keep the trees.

(B) Succeed because Jerry has a prescriptive easement that gives him a right to keep the trees.

(C) Succeed because Jerry has both an express easement and a prescriptive easement that give him a right to keep the trees.

(D) Fail because Jerry has neither an express easement nor a prescriptive easement that gives him a right to keep the trees.

In 1989, Jim and Dawn built houses on adjacent properties. State Route 10 — the only nearby highway — borders Jim's land on the west, and Dawn's property borders Jim's land on the east, so Dawn wants to be able to cross Jim's land to reach her land.

127. Her claim to an easement by necessity will always *fail* if:

(A) Dawn had offered to buy an express easement from Jim, but he refused.

(B) The land now owned by Jim and Dawn was never owned by a single person.

(C) Patricia owned all of the land now owned by Jim and Dawn until 1944, when she sold one lot to Jim and another lot to Dawn because Patricia disliked all of the traffic that the new Route 10 had generated.

(D) Dawn could reach her property by spending $700,000 to build a fifteen-mile private road across the mountains to the east of her land that connects to a dirt road that is usually open to the public.

A covenant requires Wesley Champion to maintain the inside of his townhouse "in a clean, sanitary, and attractive condition." Several visitors to Wesley's townhouse reported that his living room contains a couch upholstered in the ugliest shade of orange that they have ever seen, so the neighborhood association cited him for violating the covenant.

128. What is Wesley's best defense?

    (A) Wesley owned the couch prior to agreeing to the covenant.

    (B) The neighborhood association has acted unreasonably.

    (C) The covenant is unconstitutional.

    (D) Aesthetic concerns may only be addressed by zoning laws, not private covenants.

129. A reciprocal negative easement is created when:

    (A) A path crosses the property of two neighboring landowners so that each landowner finds it necessary to cross his neighbor's property to get to the road.

    (B) A landowner sells half of her property with the agreement that the purchaser will not use his newly bought property for residential purposes.

    (C) Nineteen out of twenty-one homeowners in a subdivision agree to paint their houses blue.

    (D) A landowner objects that her neighbor's two-story house blocks sunlight from reaching the property.

In 1999, the Natural Heritage Foundation (NHF) purchased an easement on 500 acres of wetlands owned by the Lewis family. According to the easement, it was "for the purpose of the conservation and preservation of unique and scenic areas, the environmental and ecological protection of the old growth forests, and to prevent development in a manner inconsistent with those conservation purposes." In 2002, the Lewis family sold the land to Eighteen Enterprises, which plans to build a championship golf course on 75 acres of the property. NHF objects that a golf course is inconsistent with the easement because of the introduction of chemicals used to keep the fairways green.

130. Eighteen Enterprises:

    (A) Cannot use the land without NHF's permission.

    (B) Can build and operate the golf course if it receives any necessary permits from the governmental authorities responsible for regulating old growth forests.

    (C) Can build and operate the golf course if it agrees not to use chemicals or otherwise interfere with the ecology and other environmental qualities of the land.

    (D) Is not bound by the agreement between the Lewis family and NHF.

Sally Adams lives in a house in Sycamore Woods, a new subdivision in a growing suburban area. It is the first house that she has ever owned. Sally had always wanted to plant rose bushes in front of her house, so she invited her new neighbor Beth to accompany her to the garden store to choose a dozen rose bushes. But Beth responded, "Sally, don't you know that flowers are not permitted in our front yards?" Sally and Beth dug out the paperwork containing the long list of covenants that were included on Sally's property, including a prohibition on "any flowering plants in the front yard of any property in this subdivision." Another provision in Sally's deed stated that "any violations of these covenants will be remedied by a judicial injunction as requested by the Sycamore Woods Homeowner's Association. Sally assumed that it would be easy to get permission to plant the rose bushes notwithstanding the covenant, but when she asked the president of the homeowner's association, he indicated that no exceptions were possible. Undeterred, Sally plans to file a lawsuit against the homeowner's association challenging the application of the covenant.

131. Sally will:

   (A) Succeed because she did not have actual notice of the covenant.

   (B) Succeed because the homeowner's association lacks the authority to regulate her use of her property.

   (C) Fail because she is in horizontal privity with the homeowner's association.

   (D) Fail because the covenant is reasonable.

The Willamette Presbyterian Church applied to the city's zoning board for a conditional use permit to construct a new church building. The board approved, except that it prohibited the church from holding any weddings or funerals because of the traffic that such events cause. The church's pastor protested that "weddings and funerals are central to what we do," but a board member responded, "You think you've got God on your side, you're exempt from zoning?"

132. Can the board prohibit the church from holding weddings or funerals?
ANSWER:

Joe Howard is a Vietnam War veteran who suffers from post-traumatic stress disorder and a heart condition. Both conditions have been worsened by his anxiety that his neighbors are spying on him, so he wants to construct a ten-foot high fence that blocks his property from the view of his neighbors. The local zoning ordinance, however, prohibits fences that are more than three feet high in order to achieve aesthetic uniformity in the community.

133. What is Joe's best argument that he be allowed to build the fence?
ANSWER:

Carrie Whittemore wants to build a house that is larger than that permitted on her lot by local land use regulations.

134. What should she do?
ANSWER:

Tempe, Arizona's zoning ordinance requires that all commercial signs be colored turquoise, magenta, or white. The ordinance is intended to achieve a uniform appearance consistent with the southwestern architecture in the city. Blockbuster Video wants to open a store in Tempe using its traditional blue, yellow, and white signs. The city refuses to grant Blockbuster a variance or any other exception to the colors rule, so Blockbuster sues in court.

135. Can Tempe enforce its ordinance against Blockbuster?
ANSWER:

During the nineteenth century, the federal government actively sought to dispose of as much of the land that it owned as possible. Logging, grazing, mining, and other types of resource extraction were the favored use of the public lands. By the end of the twentieth century, the federal government was much more likely to preserve the lands that it owned, or even to acquire additional lands. Recreation and wildlife habitat became much more important uses of the public lands.

136. Which theory of property best explains the changed view of appropriate use of the federally owned public lands?

ANSWER:

137. Growth controls are designed to:

(A) Preserve the existing character of a community.

(B) Keep housing prices down.

(C) Eliminate the need for traditional zoning laws.

(D) Regulate activities traditionally viewed as nuisances.

138. The public trust doctrine presupposes:

(A) The government's power of eminent domain.

(B) The ability of the government to obtain land by adverse possession.

(C) Original government ownership of land within a state.

(D) The government's ability to use its police power to protect environmental resources.

Laura Campbell owns three hundred acres in downtown Seattle on which she wants to build a new international trade complex. The original zoning ordinance would have prohibited such a building, but at Laura's request, the zoning was changed, provided that Laura promised to contribute her private security forces whenever a large convention was held anywhere in the city.

139. The decision to change the zoning can be described as:

(A) Spot zoning.

(B) Conditional rezoning.

(C) Spot zoning and conditional rezoning.

(D) Neither spot zoning nor conditional rezoning.

Since 1995, Barbara Bridges has operated a preschool for children ages four and five in a 2,000 square-foot building on the corner of Gumwood Street and Brick Road in Granger. In 1998, the Granger City Council enacted a zoning ordinance that allows only residential homes in the area containing Bridges' school.

140. Which of the following actions are likely to be permitted?

    (A) Bridges wants to use the building as a store selling children's educational software instead of as a preschool.

    (B) Bridges wants to build an extra classroom onto the preschool so that three-year-olds can enroll in the preschool.

    (C) Pat Schmidt buys the property from Bridges and wants to continue to operate the preschool.

    (D) None of the above.

141. The theory behind the existence of special exceptions in zoning law is that:

    (A) The division of land into zones in which certain uses are permitted is inherently based on generalizations for which the zoning board should have the power to grant exceptions.

    (B) Some uses are appropriate in a zone, but not at every location within the zone.

    (C) The zoning board should have the opportunity to consider any proposed new use of land.

    (D) The comprehensive plan cannot anticipate how development will actually occur within a community.

In June 2000, the City of Duga Resa enacted a zoning ordinance that prohibits any stores from being located in a certain neighborhood.

142. Which of the following stores will be able to operate as planned in that neighborhood notwithstanding the ordinance?

    (A) Al's All-Nighter, which operated from 1950 to 1994, and which is now set to reopen.

    (B) Ben's Busy Store, which has operated since 1989 but which was sold to a new owner three weeks after the ordinance became effective.

    (C) Cheryl's Shop, which has operated since 1986 and now plans to build an addition to accommodate drive-through customers.

    (D) Donna's Donuts, which had been Donna's Hardware until October 2000.

143. A zoning amendment is always invalid if:

    (A) One of the council members owns some of the land that was rezoned.

    (B) It is inconsistent with the comprehensive plan.

    (C) A court views the change as an adjudicative action rather than a legislative action.

    (D) None of the above.

In 1954, the City of South Bend enacted a zoning ordinance that divided the city into different kinds of residential, commercial, and industrial districts.

144.   Which of the following landowners is must likely to receive a variance from the ordinance?

(A)   In 1997, McDonald's purchased a lot that was zoned for residential purposes, but which is next to several other chain restaurants.

(B)   Frank O'Doul owns a lot that is zoned for single-family residences. He wants to build a three-story building containing eight apartment units. If he is unable to build apartments on the land, then he will not be able to recover his investment in the property.

(C)   Al Simmons wants to build a book store on his lot on Grape Road. He currently lives in a house on the lot, but because all of the neighboring properties now contain retail stores notwithstanding their original residential zoning classification, he proposes to tear down his house and replace it with the store.

(D)   Chuck Klein has owned a small vacant lot on the corner of First Street and Park Avenue since 1944. He would like to build a house that is similar to the others in the neighborhood, but the house would not satisfy the set back and minimum lot size provisions of the zoning ordinance.

The suburb of Freetown wants to control the presence of adult bookstores within its borders.

145.   Which of the following municipal ordinances is likely to be upheld?

(A)   An ordinance providing that no adult book store can be located within 1,000 feet of any other adult book store.

(B)   An ordinance providing that all adult book stores must be located within a five square-mile area in the northwest corner of the city.

(C)   Both of the ordinances in (a) and (b).

(D)   Neither of the ordinances in (a) or (b).

Jeff and Ann Miserocchi have found their potential dream house in Clarendon, Vermont. The only problem is that it is not really a house yet, but rather a nineteenth century barn that has been used to store agricultural equipment. According to the town's 1950 zoning law, the barn is located within an area zoned for both residential and agricultural uses. The zoning law also requires a minimum 40-foot setback from a residence to the nearest road, whereas the barn is as close as 10 feet to the road. The Miserocchi's want to make sure that they will be able to convert the barn into their dream house before they buy the property.

146.   The Miserocchi's should:

(A)   Assert that their plans constitute a nonconforming use.

(B)   Seek a variance based on undue hardship.

(C)   Ask for a special exception.

(D)   Threaten to bring a takings claim if the town does not approve their plans.

147.   Which legal device is *least likely* to preserve the habitat of an endangered species?

(A)   Eminent domain.

(B)   Private nuisance suits.

(C)   Easements.

(D)   Zoning.

148.   Which of the following zoning regulations would always be held to be invalid?

(A)   A ban on billboards.

(B)   A limitation on the number of unrelated people who may live in a house.

(C)   A prohibition on any buildings that are over thirty feet tall that is enacted by the vote of the people in an initiative.

(D)   None of the above.

The City of Bumblyburg has enacted a municipal ordinance providing that all commercial buildings must incorporate Art Deco design features approved by the city's architectural board. Jenny He wants to build a Chinese restaurant that has no trace of any Art Deco design.

149.   Her lawsuit to challenge the board's refusal to approve her plans to build the restaurant will most likely:

(A)   Fail because the ordinance contains a specific standard to be used by the board.

(B)   Fail because the chair of the board is the nation's leading architect.

(C)   Succeed because the restriction unconstitutionally limits her freedom of expression.

(D)   Succeed because the state's police power does not include the power to regulate aesthetics.

In 2000, the Lakeside Realty Corporation (LRC) purchased four acres of land from the defunct National Watch Corporation (NWC). The recent discovery on the property of dozens of drums containing hazardous chemicals that were never disposed by NWC has prompted the state to bring a public nuisance lawsuit against LRC.

150.   LRC is mostly likely to avoid liability for a public nuisance if:

(A)   It had not known about the presence of buried hazardous wastes when it bought the property.

(B)   The drums were leaking, but none of the neighbors have suffered any illnesses resulting from the contamination.

(C)   The state's environmental statutes do not regulate the storage of hazardous wastes.

(D) The drums containing the hazardous chemicals were neither leaking nor corroded.

151. Conditional rezoning is based on the belief that:

(A) The comprehensive plan must be followed in all situations.

(B) The courts are in the best position to decide when a use should be permitted.

(C) It is permissible for the legislature to enter into an agreement in which it agrees to surrender certain governmental power provided that the legislature receives a sufficient benefit in return.

(D) Flexibility is needed to allow land uses that would be appropriate in certain situations.

152. The theory justifying the use of a floating zone is:

(A) A city should be able to approve a particular use without deciding precisely where that use will occur.

(B) The zoning board must be given the authority to change its mind about the appropriate zoning in a particular area.

(C) The zoning board should be able to condition its approval of a proposed project.

(D) The area subject to a zoning ordinance must expand as the population of a metropolitan area grows.

The United States Forest Service has decided to ban logging in a 10,000 acre area of the Pacific Northwest National Forest, while permitting logging on the remaining 40,000 acres of the forest. Timber companies object to the restriction on logging in the 10,000 acre area, while environmental organizations object to logging on the 40,000 acre area.

153. The best argument for sustaining both of the Forest Service's decisions against a judicial challenge is:

(A) A landowner is allowed to exclude any unwanted uses.

(B) The Forest Service is an executive branch agency that is authorized to manage public lands as it deems best.

(C) Congress has directed the Forest Service to accommodate different types of uses.

(D) Federal courts lack jurisdiction to decide disputes concerning public lands.

In June 1999, lots of people died when car bombs exploded at the American embassies in Kenya and Tanzania. Two months later, the United States retaliated when President Clinton directed the Air Force to fire Tomahawk missiles at a pharmaceutical plant in Sudan that was suspected of engaging in terrorist operations. The missiles destroyed the plant. The owner of the plant denied any terrorist connection, and he has sued the federal government for taking his property without just compensation.

154.   Why will his lawsuit fail?

ANSWER:

Bisrat Mekuria owns the Sweet Mango Café on New Hampshire Avenue, a major street in the northeast part of Washington, D.C. In 1993, the City of Washington began building a new station on New Hampshire Avenue for the Metro subway. The construction site is directly in front of the café and is surrounded by a nine foot high fence topped with barbed wire. The postal service and the local newspaper have stopped delivering to the café, the police find it difficult to reach the area, car traffic is detoured onto other streets, and pedestrians can reach the café only if they walk 100 feet along a two-foot wide sidewalk next to the barbed wire fence. Other businesses on the street have closed, and the café has seen an 85% drop in customers. Construction is scheduled to be completed by January 1, 1999.

155.   Does the Constitution require the city to pay Mekuria any compensation?

ANSWER:

156.   How is the constitutional law of takings consistent with the idea of property as a
       bundle of sticks?

ANSWER:

In 1946, Quincy County built County Road 14 parallel to the Falcon River. The county discovered in 2002 that the road was not built on county land, as it had supposed, but rather on land owned by Russell Patterson. The county quickly moved to quiet title to the land, and in January 2003 the state supreme court held that the county had acquired title to the property by adverse possession. Now Patterson has filed a takings claim against the county in federal district court.

157. What are the county's arguments for insisting that its acquisition of the land is not a taking?

ANSWER:

Many state courts have held that the government does not have to provide compensation when the police seize private property in the course of executing a valid search warrant.

158. Why is compensation not required in such cases?

ANSWER:

The city of Santa Rosa seeks to preserve its reputation as the garden city of the southwest.

159. Toward that end, which of the following actions is the city least likely to be able to take without committing a taking of private property?

(A) The city seeks an injunction against the operation of a dry cleaning shop that is releasing chemicals that are poisoning the flowers in the city's public gardens.

(B) The city requires each developer to acquire and donate ten acres of land adjacent to the city's public gardens in order to receive approval to construct a new subdivision.

(C) The city requires all homeowners to plant on their land a small garden that contains at least one of the flowers featured in the city's public gardens.

(D) The city imposes a hotel tax that uses the revenue from those staying in hotels in the city to pay for the expansion of the city's public gardens.

160. The prevailing view of what constitutes a "public use" for purposes of the fifth amendment:

(A) Focuses on the government's means, not the government's ends.

(B) Makes the public use requirement coextensive with the police power.

(C) Holds that the government obtain title to the property.

(D) Remains unclear from the decided Supreme Court cases.

The scriptural teaching regarding land indicates that God is the original owner of all property, and that all human property owners should be stewards of the land.

161. If that view is correct, then the argument for granting the power of eminent domain to the government:

(A) Disappears because the eminent domain power can only be justified on the theory that sovereign states own all land before the land is distributed to private individuals.

(B) Assumes that the government can use land in a manner that is beneficial to the entire community.

(C) Depends upon the willingness of the government to pay for the land that it wants.

(D) Presumes that the government will only take land when it is absolutely necessary to do so.

Donna Developer wants to build a 150-story commercial and office building, a structure that would become the largest building in the world. To her dismay, she is unable to obtain a variance to the city's zoning ordinance, which limits buildings to 50 stories.

162. In her resulting takings case against the city, Donna will:

(A) Win, because of the ad coelum doctrine.

(B) Win, because concerns about the height of buildings are beyond the scope of the zoning power.

(C) Lose, because she can still use her property.

(D) Lose, because her building would be a nuisance.

Ralph Rancher owns 200 acres of rural land that has been in his family for three generations. Much to his surprise and dismay, the sprawl of a city nearly 75 miles away has begun to affect the area in which Ralph lives. Ralph's greatest concern is with a new airport that was built just three miles away from his house. The airport is used both by commercial airliners serving distant international destinations and by military jets of the United States Air Force. Airplanes now fly about 150 feet directly over his house.

163. Which of the following claims might be available to Ralph?

(A) A takings claim, but not a nuisance claim.

(B) A nuisance claim, but not a takings claim.

(C) Both a takings claim and a nuisance claim.

(D) Neither a takings claim nor a nuisance claim.

Congress is concerned that federal agencies are failing to develop adequate web sites that describe the government's work to the public. Congress is also loathe to compete with the salaries offered to web designers in the private sector. Accordingly, Congress enacts a statute authorizing agencies to use the web sites of private corporations as models for federal agency web sites. Soon thereafter, the Department of Agriculture's new web site bears an uncanny resemblance to the web site of the American Farm Association (AFA).

164. The AFA's takings claim against the federal government will:

(A) Succeed, because the federal government has used the AFA's web site without permission.

(B) Succeed, because of the congressional purpose to avoid having to hire web designers.

   (C)   Fail, because web site designs are not property within the meaning of the takings clause.

   (D)   Fail, because the AFA's web site still retains substantial value.

The national office of the American Wetlands Association (AWA) has been located on the edge of the Great Swamp since 1950. In 2003, the state took the land owned by the AWA for use as a public park.

165.   What amount of compensation is the AWA most likely to receive?

   (A) $50,000, the cost of finding land near a wetland that can be developed for the replacement of the AWA's office.

   (B) $25,000, the amount that a local real estate agent calculates that a private buyer would pay for the site.

   (C) $15,000, the typical cost of building a public park in the state.

   (D)   Nothing.

The Stodden Bridge was built in 1888 by the outlaw Butch Cassidy in order to facilitate his escape from a posse organized by railroad magnate Edward R. Harriman. This news has attracted many tourists to the area, to the delight of Aaron and Brandon, who charge visitors to use their land on either side of the bridge. But the survival of the bridge is threatened by the amount of traffic across it. Therefore, in order to protect the bridge, the Madison County commissioners enacted an ordinance prohibiting any motorized vehicles from using the Stodden Bridge. As a result, Aaron and Brandon must follow a different route to town that adds 45 minutes to their trip every day. Frustrated, Aaron and Brandon have sued the county claiming that it has taken their land without just compensation.

166.   Aaron and Brandon's takings claim will likely:

   (A)   Succeed, because the prohibition on using the bridge does not constitute a public use.

   (B)   Succeed, because fairness requires the community to share the burdens of historic preservation.

   (C)   Fail, because the government does not need to pay compensation if it is using land for historic preservation.

   (D)   Fail, because their land is still valuable.

167.   The federal government does not commit a taking when it clears navigable waterways pursuant to a navigation servitude because:

   (A)   Interferences with navigation constitute a nuisance.

   (B)   Nobody owns the land beneath navigable waterways.

   (C)   The government is exercising its property right.

   (D)   The government has already paid for the clearance itself.

168. Which of the following cases illustrates the denominator problem?

   (A) Alicia's Market purchased 20 acres of forested land in 1990, built a store on 10 acres in 1996, used seven more acres to add to the store in 1999, and is now told by the city that it cannot build on the last three acres of land because a rare salamander has just been sighted there.

   (B) The Benjamin Realty Company owns 50 acres of undeveloped land that it has been hoping to use for a shopping center, but it just learned that the entire property qualifies as wetlands that cannot be developed without a permit, and the state refuses to issue a permit for a shopping center there.

   (C) In 2001, the Community Church received a gift of 100 acres so that the church could expand its ministries. The city now wants to exercise its eminent domain power so that the 100 acres can be used for a large public recreational facility.

   (D) Dr. Davis acquired 10 acres in 2000, and she is now told by the state that she can only develop five acres if she sets aside the other five acres as wildlife habitat.

The city of Rivertown wants to redevelop its downtown waterfront area by replacing the existing abandoned factories and vacant land with retail shops and green space. One of the parcels of land that the city would like to improve is owned by the River Iron Works, which used to manufacture a variety of iron products there but which has since switched to the production of cell phones in the old factory on the land. River Iron Works wants to expand its cell phone operations by building another building on the vacant adjacent property that the company owns, but it must obtain a variety of zoning, building, and environmental permits from the city to do so. The city wants shops and parks instead of the proposed expanded cell phone operation, but the city faces a severe budgetary shortfall.

169. Which course of action is the city most likely to be able to take to achieve some of its goals?

   (A) Institute eminent domain proceedings and pay the company the fair market value of the land as a park.

   (B) Approve the project provided that the company allows shops to be built on its property in order to benefit the city's retail environment.

   (C) Approve the project provided that the company sets aside one quarter of its land that will not be built upon because of flooding concerns.

   (D) Sue the existing factory as a private nuisance because it interferes with the economic development of the city.

170. Which government action is most likely to be judged a taking of Julia's property?

   (A) A federal Environmental Protection Agency order requiring the installation of three groundwater monitoring wells on Julia's land because of concerns that the aquifer below her land has been contaminated by pesticide runoff from neighboring farms.

(B)   A state historic preservation statute that prohibits Julia from building a master bedroom suite onto her nineteenth century home.

(C)   A new county zoning amendment that designates Julia's land as residential, thus preventing Julia from realizing her longstanding plan to someday operate a bed and breakfast there.

(D)   A city health department's order to destroy Julia's building because anthrax was found there.

PRACTICE FINAL EXAM

For many years, Charlotte Welchans has owned lakefront property that she has allowed the public to use as a popular hiking destination. Charlotte is nearing retirement, though, and she needs money more than land. But she wants to make sure that the many families who have enjoyed the land for hiking continue to be able to do so. So she conveys the land "to the Lakefront Industrial Corporation so long as the public is allowed to hike on the property, then to Washington County."

171. Who owns what interest in the land?

ANSWER:

In 1988, Rock County issued a permit for Patriot Storage to operate a self-storage business that used semitrailers parked on property on Hollywood Avenue. Patriot then purchased sixteen semitrailers and placed them on the property, and soon its business was thriving. But the county revoked the permit in 2003 because a change in the county zoning ordinance prohibited the use of semitrailers for permanent storage. Patriot tried to appeal that decision, but county officials told the company that it had to sue the county instead.

172. Will Patriot's claims based upon 42 U.S.C. § 1983 succeed?

ANSWER:

Some courts have held that a landowner has a natural law right to the rainfall that occurs naturally upon that property, a right that cannot be violated by human weather modification activities.

173. How would weather modification programs fare under other theories of property?

ANSWER:

Sylvester DeFranco is a 29-year-old, internationally famous classical pianist. On February 14, he gave a sapphire ring to Hilda Stein, a former student whom he had been dating for two years. He also told her that he had chosen a new piano for her, and all she had to do was travel to the company's factory in Estonia to choose which piano she wanted. Hilda was thrilled and immediately began making plans to visit Estonia while on a spring break trip in April. Then, on February 16, Sylvester was hospitalized with an inexplicable headache. Sylvester had never missed a day of work in his life, so he assumed that he was stressed about his upcoming Carnegie Hall debut. But the doctors informed him instead that he had a cancerous tumor in his brain, and thus had only weeks to live. Shocked, Sylvester gave Hilda the deed to his Colorado mountain home. By March 1, however, the doctors realized that they had made a terrible mistake: Sylvester did not have cancer after all, but rather a very treatable allergy. Hilda, meanwhile, had given up on Sylvester and fallen in love with Sergei, the travel agent who was helping her arrange her trip to Europe. Sylvester is outraged, but Hilda insists that she gets to keep everything that he gave her.

174.   Which gifts -if any -are Hilda allowed to keep: the ring, the piano, and the home?

ANSWER:

Andrew Jackson served as President of the United States from 1828 to 1836, then he died in 1845. In 2003, the Andrew Jackson Car Wash advertised its business on the internet, replete with a likeness of Old Hickory himself. The descendants of President Jackson believe that they should be able to stop such crass exploitation.

175.   Do the policies supporting the right of publicity support their claims?

ANSWER:

Las Vegas and its nearby suburbs throughout Clark County, Nevada, have experienced phenomenal growth in recent years as a result of the casinos and related services that have made the city an international tourist destination. This growth, however, has caused many complaints about the increased traffic, pollution, crime, and cost of housing. In response to these concerns, the Nevada Legislature has just enacted the Clark County Growth Control Act of 2002 (CCGCA). According to section 1 of the CCGCA:

> "Any residential subdivisions built more than ten miles from the city center must pay an impact fee of $2,750 per residence. All moneys collected pursuant to this section will be used to pay for public roads, sewer lines, water supplies, public art, and other infrastructure provided by the county."

Big Casino Developers wants to build a subdivision on land twelve miles from the city center.

176.   Does it have to pay the impact fee?

ANSWER:

Section 2 of the CCGCA described in the preceding question provides: "No more than four unrelated persons may live in any single family house, except that as many as eight unrelated persons may live in a house that is used to aid those who suffer from a communicable disease, who are recovering from substance abuse or another disorder, or who are on parole from imprisonment." Big Casino Developers wants to contribute to the community by establishing a series of homes that each treat a group of 25 compulsive gamblers.

177. Will section 2 of the CCGCA block the developer from establishing those homes?

ANSWER:

The Acme Forest Products Company owned 20,000 acres of pristine forested land. It had hoped to harvest the timber on that land, but more stringent environmental regulations make it unlikely that the company will ever succeed in doing so. Additionally, the company's directors wanted to cultivate an environmentally progressive image. So they decided to sell the land to Celia, Suzanne, and Beth, three sisters whose family has lived in the area for generations. The deed simply stated that "these 20,000 acres are conveyed in fee simple to Celia, Suzanne, and Beth." Now, a few years later, the sisters have had a falling out resulting from their different plans for the land. Celia and Suzanne want to preserve the land in its natural state; Beth wants to build a development containing luxury vacation homes.

178. Assuming that there are no regulatory obstacles, can Beth build the development of vacation homes on the 20,000 acres without the consent of Celia and Suzanne?

ANSWER:

A. Simpson Dickson owned two urban lots that he wanted to sell, but he abhorred the idea that the land would ever be used for a coffee shop. Accordingly, Dickson conveyed the first lot "to Andrea and her heirs, but if liquor is ever sold on the premises then I or my heirs may reenter and terminate their estate." Dickson conveyed the second lot "to Andrea and her heirs, but if any of them ever allow the operation of a coffee shop on this land, then to Boris and his heirs." Thirty years later, Dickson died. Then, without reading the original deeds, Andrea's sole heir Joyce opened a coffee shop that spans both lots.

179. Who owns the right to possess each lot?

ANSWER:

In 1960, two neighboring landowners — Mom's Family Restaurant and the Speedy Gas Station — entered into a covenant pursuant to which "Speedy and its successors agree to only sell such food as is provided in vending machines" on its property. Ten years later, Mom's Family Restaurant sold its land to Food Now, a franchise which has operated a fast-food restaurant on the property ever since then. In 2000, Speedy sold its land to Global Food & Oil, which wants to operate a convenience store along with selling gas. Food Now objects because it does not want to lose any business.

180. Does the original covenant prohibit Global from operating a convenience store?

ANSWER:

The Friendly General Store and the First Baptist Church own adjoining lots in the center of town. In 1944, the church built a new building for its growing congregation. In 1980, the general store began experiencing problems arising from leaking water, which the store soon traced to water falling from the overhanging gutters of the church. A survey of the lands determined that the roof of the church extends four feet across the boundary between the land owned by the parties.

181. Is the church liable for a trespass?

ANSWER:

In 1989, Juanita died with a will leaving her land "to the Covenant Community Church so long as the property is used for private Christian education, then to the American Cancer Society." The church built a school there which it operated for twelve years. Then, in response to the school's need to expand, the church sold the land to the Pleasant Hills Homeowner's Association, which began to build a country club on the property. The country club was almost complete when the provision in the original deed was discovered.

182. Who owns the land?

ANSWER:

The Hatfield family's home is next door to the McCoy family's home.

183. Which of the following activities are the Hatfields allowed to engage in?

(A) The Hatfields may walk across the middle of the McCoys' property if they obtained an easement from the McCoys' predecessors.

(B) The Hatfields may walk across the corner of the McCoys' property so long as they do not cause *any* damage to their property.

(C) The Hatfields may operate a brick kiln on their property even though the fumes poison the McCoy children.

(D) The Hatfields may build a swimming pool in their backyard even though the excavation will cause the McCoys' house to subside.

The Standard Realty Company (SRC) owns a house in the town of Southchester that it rented to four families who immigrated to the United States from Puerto Rico in 1998. The house was built in 1960. In 1977, the town changed the zoning of the property from residential to light industrial. In 1999, in response to a complaint from the neighbors, the town investigated and cited SRC with violating the provisions of the municipal zoning ordinance that allow only one family to live in each home in areas that are zoned residential. SRC did not take any action in response to that citation. Then, in 2001, the house was struck by lightning and burned to the ground. SRC wants to rebuild the house, but the town has refused to issue a permit.

184.   SRC's lawsuit against the city will likely:

   (A)   Succeed based upon the Fair Housing Act's prohibition against discrimination.

   (B)   Succeed because zoning restrictions based upon family status are unconstitutional.

   (C)   Fail because SRC's failure to remedy the violation of the occupancy limit estops SRC from objecting to future zoning decisions.

   (D)   Fail because a nonconforming use cannot be replaced once it is destroyed.

The law firm of Edwin & Hilles owns a 50-story office tower in downtown Metropolis. In 1996, the city built a large sports stadium on the neighboring land. The city allowed Edwin & Hilles to build a pedestrian walkway from the tenth floor of their office tower -which contains retail stores and restaurants -to the stadium entrance. In 2002, however, concerns about security prompted the city to permanently block the walkway at the stadium entrance.

185.   If Edwin & Hilles bring a takings claim against the city, that claim will fail because:

   (A)   A sports stadium is a public use.

   (B)   The state's police power allows the government to act in response to concerns about security.

   (C)   The government can take an easement without triggering the duty to pay just compensation.

   (D)   Edwin & Hilles cannot establish an implied easement.

Late one night, Paula Paparazzi tracked down a famous politician and an equally famous movie star as they engaged in a romantic encounter in a secluded part of a public beach. Paula took several dozen photographs of their indiscretions. Then, as they left, Paula noticed that something had fallen from the movie star's neck onto the sand. Paula waited until they were a safe distance away, ran to the spot where they had been, and picked up the locket that was sitting there. The locket contained the seal of the United States Senate, and it was inscribed, "For Lucretia, my lover, from your favorite Senator." The locket was tarnished, though, so Paula wanted to clean it before she publicized the relationship that she had discovered. So Paula took the locket to the nearby StuffMart, which included a counter that promised to polish any jewelry at any time, day or night. Paula dropped off the locket, left for an hour to get something to eat, and returned for the polished locket. But when she arrived at the counter in the StuffMart, there was a "closed until the morning" sign there. A few days later, Paula was horrified to learn that the locket was being advertised for sale at StuffMart. Paula immediately drove to the store and demanded the locket back. But Lucretia and the Senator had learned of the locket by this time, and they each demanded it, too.

186. Who owns the locket?

    (A) The Senator.

    (B) Lucretia.

    (C) Paula.

    (D) StuffMart.

The Flying A gas station has stood on the corner of Park Avenue and Roosevelt Road since 1940. In 2000, the city enacted an ordinance that zoned the area for residential purposes only.

187. The gas station is most likely to be able to remain as a nonconforming use even though:

    (A) The building returned to use as a gas station in 2000 after having been a video store during the two previous years.

    (B) The building has always been used as a gas station, but the storage tanks buried on the property have contaminated the neighborhood's water supply.

    (C) The city plans to exercise its power of eminent domain to buy the property and close the gas station.

    (D) The gas station attracts so many cars that the site becomes out of character for the neighborhood.

188. Which of the following animals is most likely to be lawfully possessed by the Robinson family?

    (A) Hoppy, a Florida Keys marsh rabbit that the family has cared for as a pet since they read that such rabbits are listed under the federal Endangered Species Act.

    (B) Bambi, a deer that the family rescued from a hunter whose shot had wounded it and who was about to kill the deer.

    (C) Simba, a Labrador retriever who lives with the family in their home in Rhode Island, where a state statute refers to pets as companions instead of as being owned.

    (D) Al, a donkey that lives on the family's property in a part of the county that is zoned to forbid landowners from keeping any animals.

Acme, Inc., operates a landfill next to the home of Julia Coleman. Julia sues Acme alleging that the landfill constitutes a private nuisance. The court agrees and issues an injunction against the landfill.

189. Acme can respond in each of the following ways *except*:

    (A) Insisting that the government pay for an inverse condemnation of the landfill.

    (B) Closing the landfill.

    (C) Modifying the operation of the landfill.

    (D) Paying Julia to settle the case.

190. Which landlord is most likely to regain possession of his property from the current tenant?

    (A) Allen, who declined to renew his tenant Anthony's apartment lease for a tenancy at will when Allen discovered that Anthony had posted complaints about the apartment on the city housing department's web site.

    (B) Bryce, who leased farmland to Boyd for one year based on Boyd's local reputation as an excellent hog farmer, and who objects to Boyd's plan to sublease the property to a college friend who wants to live in the country for a while.

    (C) Celia, who leased a house to Chris with explicit notice of the house's many failings, and who now seeks to evict Chris, who refuses to pay the rent until Celia fixes the pipes to provide water to the home.

    (D) Deborah, who rented office space to David, a doctor who refuses to pay the rent because the noise from the city hospital next door makes it impossible for him to work there.

In 2002, Linda Klein Jackson died with a will leaving her lake home "to Andrew for life, then to such of the grandchildren of Andrew who reach the age of 21." At the time of Linda's death, Andrew was 43 years old, and he had two daughters Katy and Christina.

191. Upon Linda's death, Andrew owned which interest in the lake home?

    (A) Life estate.

    (B) Life estate subject to condition subsequent.

    (C) Fee simple.

    (D) Fee simple subject to condition subsequent.

Greg Jones has suffered from alcoholism since he was in a car accident nearly twenty years ago. In August 1999, he purchased a unit in the Pacific Vistas condominiums near the beach in Carmel, California. As part of the purchase, he signed an agreement containing a covenant stating that "the owner shall keep the premises free of any pornographic materials." Shortly after Greg moved in, two children playing in an adjacent yard notified their parents that they had seen Jeff viewing pornographic web sites while surfing the internet on his porch. The Pacific Vistas Homeowner's Association -of which his unit is a part -has fined Jeff $1,000 for violating the covenant.

192. Greg's argument against paying the fine will likely:

(A) Succeed, because the covenant is unconstitutional.

(B) Succeed, because the enforcement of the covenant would violate the federal Fair Housing Act.

(C) Fail, because his conduct was seen by the children.

(D) Fail, if the state makes it illegal to possess pornography.

193. The federal government must pay just compensation if it:

(A) Destroys a company's factory because it has been contaminated by anthrax.

(B) Denies a company's permit application to explore for oil in the Arctic National Wildlife Refuge.

(C) Places captive-born grizzly bears on federal lands in Idaho, only to watch those bears wander onto a nearby private ranch and eat the sheep there.

(D) Uses a company's trade secret in order to produce a new anti-ballistic missile system.

In 1999, William Aldridge drafted a will devising his farm "to Lance and Paula as joint tenants." In December 2001, Lance died. Two weeks later, William died.

194. Who owns the farm?

(A) Paula.

(B) Lance's heirs and Paula as tenants in common.

(C) Lance's heirs and Paula as joint tenants.

(D) William's heirs.

195. Which of the following can be established implicitly rather than explicitly?

(A) A tenancy at will.

(B) A real covenant.

(C) A homeowner's association's recreational fee.

(D) A zoning variance.

196. Jeremy Bentham's utilitarian theory of property implies that:

(A) The federal Wilderness Act is ill-conceived because it prevents human use of land.

(B) The Visual Artists Rights Act is based upon the improper premise that natural rights determine property.

(C) Local zoning laws are invalid because they rest upon an arbitrary community judgment about how to use property.

  (D) Reforms in landlord and tenant law are misguided to the extent that they rely upon contract law principles.

The oil spill from the *Exxon Valdez* into the Prince Georges Sound caused a variety of injuries to the Alaskan tourist industry, to the fisheries located in the area, and to the native Alaskans who engaged in a subsistence lifestyle on their land near the site.

197. Which of the following lawsuits brought by the native Alaskans against Exxon is most likely to succeed?

  (A) A private nuisance action alleging that the native Alaskans are afraid to eat the fish from the sound even though scientists insist that they have nothing to fear.

  (B) A private nuisance action seeking damages for lost income.

  (C) A public nuisance action alleging that the native Alaskans are afraid to eat the fish from the sound even though scientists insist that they have nothing to fear.

  (D) A public nuisance action seeking damages for lost income.

Dr. Gomez is a medical researcher who developed a new stem cell line. One of his students was jealous of Gomez, so he destroyed all of Gomez's work.

198. If Gomez sues the student for conversion, Gomez will:

  (A) Win, because the stem cell line is property protected by a conversion action.

  (B) Lose, because the stem cell line is not property.

  (C) Lose, because a conversion action is not allowed in such circumstances.

  (D) Lose, both because the stem cell line is not property and because a conversion action is not allowed in such circumstances

At their high school graduation, Laura wanted to give her favorite old doll to her best friend Julia. Julia said thanks, but she insisted that she was not interested in taking such a valuable childhood treasure from Laura. Laura pleaded with Julia to think about it, so they sat the doll on a public bench as they entered a nearby restaurant for dinner. During dinner, Laura convinced Julia to keep the doll. Only then did they realize that they did not have it. They looked everywhere and asked everyone in the building, but no one remembered seeing the doll. Nor did anyone respond to the notices that they posted around the school and near the restaurant. Instead, one week later, a friend of Julia's saw the doll up for auction online. Julia contacted Ellen, the seller, who said that she found the doll in the trash outside the building where Laura and Julia had left it. Ellen refused to return the doll, and Margaret won the online auction.

199. Who is the owner of the doll?

  (A) Laura.

  (B) Julia.

  (C) Ellen.

(D) Margaret.

The Comprehensive Environmental Response Compensation and Liability Act (CERCLA) of 1980 is a federal statute that holds landowners liable for the cost of cleaning up hazardous wastes that are in danger of escaping from their property, even if the current landowner did not introduce the wastes to the property.

200. The best common law analogy to such liability is found in:

    (A) Private nuisance law.

    (B) Public nuisance law.

    (C) Trespass law.

    (D) Negligence principles of tort law.

In 2002, Acme Realty leased a commercial office building to Tracy for ten years at a rent of $15,000 per month. The lease states that "the tenant shall not assign or sublease these premises." Last week, Glen offered to pay Tracy $50,000 per month if she would transfer her interest in the building to him to use for his rapidly expanding dot com company. Glen is 26 years old, a recent millionaire, and notable for his many tattoos. Acme, however, objects to Glen's presence in the building.

201. Which is of the following statements of the law is most likely to be correct?

    (A) Acme cannot block the transfer because it is neither an assignment nor a sublease.

    (B) Acme would violate the Fair Housing Act if it objected to Glen's presence because of his tattoos.

    (C) Acme cannot block the transfer, but it can require Tracy to pay Acme the $35,000 additional rent that Glen is willing to pay.

    (D) Acme can block the transfer based on its opposition to dot com companies.

The Long Acres Development Corporation (LADC) owned 199 acres of farmland that it planned to subdivide for a new housing development. On June 1, 2000, LADC conveyed Lot 43 to the Van Burens as joint tenants. Four months later, and for a much higher price, LADC conveyed Lot 43 to Emily Harrison. The Van Burens did not record their deed, and Emily had no reason to know of the earlier conveyance, so Emily recorded her deed immediately upon receiving it. Then, in March 2003, Emily sold Lot 43 to Hugh Thomas, who already owned the neighboring Lot 42. Thomas knew that the Van Burens had purchased Lot 43 in 2000, but he declined to tell Emily or anyone else about these events. Instead, he simply recorded the deed that he received from Emily. Soon thereafter, the Van Burens arrived with a building contractor to plan their new home, only to be greeted by another contractor who was working for Hugh.

202. Who owns Lot 43?

    (A) LADC

(B) The Van Burens.

(C) Emily.

(D) Hugh.

The attorney for the Amber Realty Company argued that "[e]ven if the world could agree by unanimous consent what is beautiful and desirable, it could not, under our constitutional theory, enforce its decision by prohibiting a land owner, who refuses to accept the world's view of beauty, from making otherwise safe and innocent uses of his land."

203. The Supreme Court rejected that argument in *Village of Euclid v. Ambler Realty Co.*, 272 U.S. 325 (1926), because:

(A) The Court reviewed the record and found as a matter of fact that the company's proposed use of its land was not "otherwise safe and innocent."

(B) The judgment of the Euclid village council was entitled to deference.

(C) Nothing in the Constitution protects a property owner from a government land use regulation that is intended to provide for the public good.

(D) The company had to abide by the popular majority's view of beauty.

204. Which of the following acts is permitted by the Fair Housing Act?

(A) A suburban family refuses to rent its house to a man because the man is from China.

(B) A developer refuses to rent an apartment to a white college student because the developer wants to maintain a racially integrated building.

(C) An apartment owner advertises in a local newspaper indicating that only women will be considered to live in vacant units.

(D) A developer refuses to sell a house in a new subdivision that he has just constructed to an Episcopal priest because the developer wants to create a community that is comprised of 100 Jewish families.

Jack and Jill were married in a community property state, and they are now getting divorced there. Before they were married, Jill accumulated nearly $80,000 in student loans which they paid together while they were married. They also bought a house as joint tenants while they were married, and they acquired a credit card account which they both used. Now that they are separated, Jill continues to live in the house.

205. Which of the following liabilities is Jill alone most likely to have to pay?

(A) The student loan payments.

(B) The debt on the credit card.

(C) The mortgage on the house.

(D) Rent for continuing to live in the house.

Brady Village is a residential development consisting of 200 homes. When the development was built in 1967, each of the lots contained a covenant limiting the use of the land to single-family residences.

206. Which action is most likely to make the covenant unenforceable?

(A) The city council considers a proposal to rezone the area for commercial uses.

(B) There are many other alternative residential developments nearby.

(C) Twenty-two residents of the development run offices out of their homes.

(D) Each lot is worth $75,000 for residential purposes and $550,000 for commercial purposes.

Andy stole a watch from Betsy, who bought it from Cara, who found it on a counter in the Dickens grocery store, where it was left by Esther, who inherited it from her grandmother. The police recovered the watch when they arrested Andy, but Esther has no idea what happened to the watch despite repeated efforts of the police, Cara, Betsy, and the Dickens grocery store to identify the original owner.

207. Which of these parties has the best claim to own the watch?

(A) Andy.

(B) Betsy.

(C) Cara.

(D) The Dickens grocery store.

In September 1994, Oscar Ornithologist asked Helga Habitat for permission to use her property to watch the annual migration of the spectacular but endangered whooping crane. Helga said that would be fine. One year later, Oscar asked Helga if he could use the land to watch the whooping cranes again, this time accompanied by a couple dozen members of the local Audubon Society. Again, Helga agreed. For the next several years, Oscar kept asking for permission to bring larger and larger groups onto the land, and Helga kept agreeing. Finally, on September 1, 2002, Oscar called Helga on her cell phone and asked her to allow the 5,000 participants in the Audubon Society's annual national convention to use her land for one week during each of the next five years. Helga said yes. Oscar then spent $100,000 of his own money to advertise the event and to secure non-refundable deposits for the few hotel rooms in the area. But on the day before the event, Helga changed her mind and refused to let anyone on her land.

208. Oscar and the convention participants have:

(A) An express easement.

(B) An easement by necessity.

(C) An easement by estoppel.

(D) No right to use Helga's land.

209. Which of the following laws is most likely to encourage private developers to build more housing for low-income residents?

    (A) The federal Fair Housing Act.

    (B) State statutes protecting the habitat of rare wildlife.

    (C) Local zoning ordinances containing minimum lot size requirements.

    (D) Common law implied warranties of habitability.

In March 2002, Jennifer Young purchased ten acres of land from the Suburban Development Corporation (SDC). She did not record her purchase. In November 2002, Jennifer's ex-husband Matthew purchased the same ten acres from SDC, knowing that Jennifer had already purchased that land. Matthew immediately recorded his deed to the property.

210. Matthew owns the land according to a jurisdiction following:

    (A) The common law rule.

    (B) A race statute.

    (C) A notice statute.

    (D) A race-notice statute.

211. Which zoning ordinance is least likely to be upheld?

    (A) An ordinance that prohibits adjacent adult bookstores, with a 25-year amortization period.

    (B) An ordinance that prohibits more than two people from living in any apartment unit.

    (C) An ordinance in a wealthy suburb that zones 20% of the land for houses that cost at least $500,000 each, and 20% of the land for apartments.

    (D) An ordinance that allows commuter train stations in residential zones but does not allow banks in residential zones.

Juan Martinez wants to dispose of most of his property holdings before he retires from his job as a real estate agent. Toward that end, Juan sells twenty acres of undeveloped land "to Angela so long as it is not developed during her lifetime, then to Bob's widow and her heirs." At the time of the conveyance, Angela is 56 years old, Bob is 72 years old, and Bob's wife Elizabeth is 70 years old.

212. Angela owns:

    (A) A fee simple absolute.

    (B) A fee simple determinable.

    (C) A life estate.

    (D) No interest in the property.

Janice has just moved to College Town, where she is in her first year of graduate school. She would like to live in a house owned by CT Realty because of a friend's recommendation and because of its proximity to her classes. In fact, she was so desperate to live in the house that she agreed to start paying $900 per month rent while she worked on a formal lease with CT Realty. After a few weeks, though, Janice and CT Realty were unable to agree upon a formal lease.

213. How long can Janice stay in the house?

(A) She must leave immediately.

(B) She must leave when CT Realty asks her to.

(C) She can stay so long as she pays $900 per month rent to CT Realty.

(D) She can stay for the current school year.

On January 15, 2001, Lucy Landlord leased her farm to Calvin Swine for a period of three years. On January 15, 2002, Calvin entered into an agreement with Donna Developer in which Calvin "subleases, transfers, and assigns" his interest in the farm to Donna for one year. By December 2002, neither Calvin nor Donna had paid any rent to Lucy for over six months.

214. Which remedies are available to Lucy?

(A) She can sue Calvin for rent, but she cannot evict Donna.

(B) She can sue Calvin for rent, or she can evict Donna.

(C) She cannot sue Calvin for rent, nor can she evict Donna.

(D) She cannot sue Calvin for rent, but she can evict Donna.

During the nineteenth century, surgery was always a highly dangerous medical procedure because patients could die of shock from the trauma of the operation, wholly unrelated to the ailment which occasioned the operation. Then Dr. Morton began to use ether vapor to anaesthetize patients during surgical operations. Morton thus applied for, and received, a patent. Undeterred, the New York Eye Infirmary started to use ether vapor as an anesthetic during its surgical procedures.

215. Morton's suit for infringement of a patent will:

(A) Succeed, because the infirmary failed to challenge the patent when it was issued.

(B) Succeed, if no one had thought about using ether as an anesthetic before he did.

(C) Fail, if the effect of ether when inhaled was obvious.

(D) Fail, because the common law does not grant inventors the exclusive right to their inventions.

The Islamic Center owns fifty acres of land in the town of Mount Davis. In 1990, the Islamic Center applied for a conditional use permit that would allow the construction of a mosque.

The town granted the permit subject to the condition that the Islamic Center not build an elementary school on the property. By 2002, the Islamic Center was interested in building a soup kitchen on its property adjacent to the mosque. The neighboring residents opposed such a soup kitchen, though, explaining at a public hearing that several sites in other parts of the town would be more appropriate for a homeless shelter and that "there are already enough of these people around here anyway." The town denied a permit for the soup kitchen for the stated reason that "services for the homeless are best provided by local governmental authorities."

216. The best claim for the Islamic Center's challenge to that decision relies upon:

(A) The limits of the police power in authorizing the application of zoning ordinances.

(B) The federal Fair Housing Act.

(C) The federal Religious Land Use and Institutionalized Persons Act.

(D) The free exercise clause of the first amendment to the United States Constitution.

217. Capture or possession is most likely to determine property rights to each of following *except*:

(A) Animals.

(B) Natural gas.

(C) Rivers subject to riparian rights.

(D) Rivers subject to prior appropriation.

218. Which property is the law most likely to allow to be destroyed?

(A) A patented machine.

(B) A famous sculpture.

(C) An historic theater.

(D) A pet cat.

The village of Rico just enacted a new zoning ordinance. The zones established by that ordinance were selected by the village council for the sole purpose of improving the quality of life -and economic well-being -of Rico's mayor. Pursuant to the new zoning scheme, a quiet retirement community suddenly discovers that a huge regional shopping center is being built on what had been the park across the street.

219. The best advice for the angry residents of the retirement community is:

(A) Sue to enjoin the shopping center as a nuisance.

(B) Contest the power of the village to engage in zoning.

(C) File a takings case.

(D)   Petition to change the zoning ordinance by popular initiative.

Barbara Bambi lives in a house outside of Portland, Oregon, next to a state wildlife area. The wildlife area hosts hundreds of deer, but since the deer do not recognize the local property boundaries, many of the deer stray onto some of the private land outside the wildlife area. Barbara likes to feed the deer that come onto her land, and her seven-year-old daughter Betty adores the deer more than anything else in the world. Next door to the Bambis, though, lives Vince Venison. Venison sees the deer as an opportunity to get rich selling gourmet meat to connoisseurs throughout the Pacific Northwest. Moreover, Venison delights in torturing the deer before he kills them. Venison tortures and kills the deer in an open area in his back yard, only twenty yards from the border between his property and Bambi's. Barbara and Betty can see everything that Venison does because their kitchen, dining room, and family room all contain big picture windows that look out into their backyard. They can also hear the terrified screams of the deer as they are being killed. Barbara hates the sight and sound of Venison's activities. She is embarrassed to invite any of her friends or family to her home because of what they might see or hear outside. Betty has been so traumatized by the sight and sound of the tortured deer that she hides in her room and has to receive psychological counseling. Barbara has asked the local government authorities to do something about Venison, but they have responded that while cruelty to animals is a misdemeanor under Oregon law, they have more important things to do than prosecute Venison. As a last resort, Barbara and Betty have filed suit asking the state court to enjoin Venison's activities as a private nuisance.

220.   Their suit will:

(A)   Succeed, because Venison does not have a permit for his actions.

(B)   Succeed, because the injuries they have suffered are redressable by nuisance law.

(C)   Fail, because the injuries they have suffered are not redressed by nuisance law.

(D)   Fail, because a private nuisance suit cannot proceed if the government's regulatory authorities have declined to act in the case.

ANSWERS

1. The Restatement definition emphasizes that the key to property is a relationship, whereas the colloquial definition presupposes a single meaning of ownership. The idea of property as the relation of people to a thing allows for a variety of such relationships. That, in turn, draws upon the concept of property rights as a bundle of sticks. Just as the precise sticks which are contained in the bundle may vary and yet still be termed "property," so too the relation of people to a thing can differ and still qualify as property.

2. One's vote for President is property within the meaning of the Restatement's understanding of "legal relations between persons with respect to a thing." A person has a right to use his or her vote, to not use that vote, and a right to possess that vote. By contrast, a person does not have a right to modify that vote, to sell his vote, or to transfer the vote to someone else even if no money exchanges hands.

3. **Answer D is the correct answer.** The occupancy theory applies to property that has never been owned, or that is no longer owned by anyone. The rule that finders are allowed to keep abandoned property is a perfect illustration of the occupancy theory.

   Answer A is incorrect because the landowner does not get to keep the new land. The occupancy theory would suggest that the first person to possess the new land would be able to own it. **Answer B is incorrect** because the right of publicity either follows from the labor theory of property, which rewards those who create new property by their labor, or perhaps by a natural rights theory that acknowledges skill in acting as a gift with which the actress was born. **Answer C is incorrect** because the right to share in a spouse's income does not derive from the "taking possession of that which at the moment is the property of no man," in Henry Maine's class definition of the occupancy theory. Instead, such marital property rules depend upon either a utilitarian, natural rights theory, or perhaps a labor theory of property.

4. **Answer B Is the correct answer.** An anticommons refers to property which a number of people control, and thus many people have the right to exclude others or to veto a transfer. An anticommons is thus the antithesis of a commons, which is property for which no one has the right to exclude. An unanimous consent requirement in a common interest community illustrates property whose use and transfer is subject to approval by multiple parties.

   Answer A is incorrect because public lands are the quintessential example of a commons, not an anticommons. Anyone can use the public lands; no one has the right to exclude others from the public lands. **Answer C is incorrect** because a wedding ring is personal property which is unlikely to be owned concurrently by more than one person. **Answer D is incorrect** because the shipwreck will either belong to its finder, the original owner, or perhaps a government claiming sovereignty over that part of the ocean. The shipwreck need not, however, be owned by multiple parties each of whose approval is required with respect to any use or transfer of the property.

5. **Answer C is the correct answer**. A number of states have statutes that empower a licensed casino to regulate those who demonstrate what is judged an unfair ability to win at various games. Such regulations are plainly within the police power of the state, as demonstrated by the long line of cases describing various gaming activities as a public nuisance.

    Answer A is incorrect because the traditional common law placed relatively few limits upon public accommodations. None of those limits, moreover, contradicted the original treatment of gambling as a public nuisance. **Answer B is incorrect** because gambling is usually regulated by the state, not local governments responsible for zoning. And even if a local government uses its zoning law to regulate the location of casinos, zoning laws are unlikely to address questions such as the rights of casinos to exclude unwanted patrons. **Answer D is incorrect** because while federal civil rights laws offer guarantees with respect to public accommodations, those guarantees are only offered to special categories of people whom the law protects from discrimination. Gamblers generally, and card-counters in particular, are not protected by federal civil rights laws.

6. **Answer C is the correct answer**. The labor theory of property teaches that property should belong to the person who is responsible for creating it. Trademark law is designed to protect the businesses who have cultivated goodwill among their customers and within the community more generally by virtue of the practices and products of that business. State anti-dilution statutes protect trademarks by imposing liability upon anyone who "dilutes" that mark by tarnishing the brand's name or otherwise suggesting that the business associated with the trademark is less savory than the public had previously believed. Thus state anti-dilution laws protect the labor that businesses expend to cultivate the goodwill associated with their trademarks.

    Answer A is incorrect because the rule of finders only sometimes rewards labor. By definition, a finder is not the creator of the property. A finder may nonetheless expend significant labor to discover property that has been lost or abandoned. For example, a professional organization dedicated to finding valuable shipwrecks certainly illustrates how a finder may exert substantial labor to recover property. But many other finders discover the property by happenstance, spotting a ring on a shelf or a bundle of money in the woods. The labor theory of property does not really apply with respect to such finders. Likewise, **Answer B is incorrect** because municipal prohibitions on spot zoning are designed to prevent favored landowners from obtaining specialized treatment, a theory which only indirectly relates to the labor (or not) that the landowner has exercised. **Answer D is incorrect** because the federal Wilderness Act protects land from human disturbances, thereby actively discouraging labor directed at that land.

7. **Answer B is the correct answer.** The public trust doctrine teaches that some property is of such importance that the public retains a trust to the land. Private owners may acquire land subject to the public trust doctrine, but the owner will own the land subject to the rights of the public to use it or to protect it from certain harms. For example, the New Jersey courts have held that beachfront property is subject to the public trust doctrine so that a private owner of such property cannot exclude the public from crossing it to get to the beach. *See Matthews v. Bay Head Improvement Ass'n*, 471 A.2d 355 (N.J.), *cert. denied*, 469 U.S. 821 (1984). The public trust doctrine thus conforms to the scriptural indication that landowners should be willing to let others use their land.

Answer A is incorrect because a tenancy at sufferance is a leasehold estate that can be ended at any time (subject to notice requirements). A tenancy at sufferance allows a tenant to remain on the landlord's property after a formal lease has expired, but the tenancy does not seek to discourage the new leasehold if the landlord chooses to do so. **Answer C is incorrect** because the touch and concern requirement determines whether a covenant runs with the land, and such covenants refer to restrictions upon land use rather than a right to let others use the land. **Answer D is incorrect** because spot zoning prohibitions bear little relation to whether others will be allowed to use the affected land. Spot zoning often benefits a small parcel of land, and that benefit attaches to the landowner regardless of the owner's willingness to make the land available to others.

8. **Answer A is the correct answer.** The Visual Artists Rights Act (VARA) of 1990 is a statute enacted by Congress to implement the provisions of the Boerne Convention. That treaty, in turn, embodies the French concept of the "moral rights" possessed by artists. These moral rights are an example of the application of a natural rights theory of property.

Answer B is incorrect because VARA operates to limit the rights of a landowner. For example, a landowner may be unable to remove a statue or sculpture if that artwork qualifies for the protections of VARA. **Answer C is incorrect** because the rights accorded by VARA are not of limited duration. **Answer D is incorrect** because VARA does not apply equally to all artwork. To the contrary, VARA only protects artwork that is significant. The law thus requires a judgment about the worthiness of art before the law protects it.

9. **Answer A is the correct answer.** The law of avulsion states that land which is added to waterfront property as the result of a sudden action such as a hurricane or an earthquake does not become the property of the riparian owner. Instead, land added by avulsion belongs to the government. This is so even though the riparian landowner is likely to have treated the new land exactly like the preexisting land, by possessing them both alike.

Answer B is incorrect because land created by accretion does belong to the riparian owner. Accretion results from the gradual, imperceptible addition of land to the waterfront property already owned by the riparian owner. Possession does produce ownership in such circumstances. **Answer C is incorrect** because the law of accession, which addresses property that has been accidentally confused or mixed together, determines ownership based upon the equitable circumstances of particular cases. Possession may result in ownership of property obtained by accession, but it may not, too. **Answer D is incorrect** because adverse possession is the best illustration of the law determining ownership based upon possession, even possession that displaces the original owner.

10. **Answer A is the correct answer**. A government job qualifies as property for purposes of the due process clause if the government gives the employee assurances of continued employment or if it limits dismissal from that job to specific reasons. In either event, due process mandates that specific procedures be afforded before the job is terminated. It is possible that the university afforded Cooper the necessary procedures, but the question here is simply whether Cooper had a protected property interest in the first place.

   Answer B is incorrect because you do not have a constitutionally protected property interest in a job which you have not been offered. **Answer C is incorrect** because while some government benefits may qualify as property within the scope of the due process clause, Cooper will probably be said to have only a "mere expectancy" in benefits that have just been established and which he has never received. **Answer D is incorrect** because the Coopers do not have a right to keep the mountain lion without a permit. The lion is thus contraband, not property.

11. **Answer B is the correct answer**. Utilitarian theory posits that the idea of property is a human construction that depends solely upon societal needs. Clay's remark captures that idea precisely.

   By contrast, natural rights theory insists that property exists independent of any given society's declarations, so **Answer A is incorrect**. **Answer C is incorrect** because Clay's statement ignores any role that human labor plays in creating that which the law regards as property. **Answer D is incorrect**, too, because Clay's statement of the nature of property does not contain an economic component, either.

12. **Answer C is the correct answer**. The public accommodations provisions of state civil rights statutes limit the ability of landowners to exclude certain members of the public from hotels, restaurants, and the like.

   By contrast, **Answer A is incorrect** because the federal trademark act gives a trademark holder the exclusive right to use a trademark, and anyone else's unlicensed use of the mark constitutes trademark infringement. **Answer B is incorrect** because state riparian rights to water extend to riparian owners of the waterbody, and those owners are entitled to exclude anybody whose actions would interfere with those rights. **Answer D is incorrect** because municipal historic preservation ordinances restrict the modification of historic properties, but such ordinances do not limit the ability of the property's owner to exclude others.

13. Werner probably owns the stamps. Werner's mother Bennie was the true owner of the stamps, and she left all of her property to Werner. Accordingly, Werner will succeed to his mother's interest in the stamps as their true owner. The only way in which Werner would lose is if Bennie is judged to have abandoned the stamps. If the stamps were abandoned, then Larry would probably get to keep them as the finder. But abandonment occurs only if there is a voluntary, knowing relinquishment of the property rights. Bennie's actions do not seem to meet that high threshold. She did not spend a lot of time looking for the stamps, but she assumed that they were lost, and she did not know where they might have fallen out of her purse. It is possible that her failure to search for the stamps more diligently could constitute an abandonment of them, but it is more likely that the court will treat the stamps as lost, and thus subject to her return as the true owner.

14. Yes, Peet can recover the value of the ring from the hotel. The facts here are drawn from *Peet v. The Roth Hotel Co.*, 253 N.W. 546 (Minn. 1934), where the court held that the hotel was liable for negligence as a bailment for hire. The hotel was a bailment for hire because it received a reciprocal benefit from keeping the ring: the service was for the benefit of its guests, and the hotel benefited from their continued patronage. As a bailment for hire, the hotel owed a duty of reasonable care that would be breached by ordinary negligence. The hotel cashier's failure to care for such an obviously valuable item constituted negligence, so the hotel was liable to Peet.

15. Charlie will probably not get the laptop. To be legally effective, Arthur's gift to Charlie required both intent and delivery. Arthur intended to give the laptop to Charlie, but Arthur did not deliver the laptop to Charlie. Arthur appears to have decided after he took the bar exam to give the laptop to Charlie, and it further appears that the laptop had already been shipped. Nonetheless, delivery to Charlie never occurred, and nothing in these events would eliminate the delivery requirement. Charlie cannot get the gift as a gift causa mortis, either, because Arthur was not under an apprehension of death when he agreed to give the laptop to Charlie.

16. An engagement ring is a conditional gift. Nonetheless, there are at least three theories as to why Brenda should be able to keep the ring that Eddie gave to her even after they decided not to get married. First, the condition attached to the gift could be viewed as Brenda's promise to marry Eddie, and since Brenda made such a promise, she is entitled to keep the ring. Second, the law could consider the circumstances in which the engagement was ended and allow Brenda to keep the ring because it was Eddie who called off the wedding. Third, a more general policy argument asserts that women bear the brunt of broken engagements, and a rule that requires the return of gifts would violate public policy by having a disproportionate impact upon women.

17. **Answer A is the correct answer**. The traditional common law rule held that the finder of a treasure trove got to keep it regardless of where it was found. In other words, even a trespasser could acquire good title to a treasure trove found on someone else's property. The incentive that such a rule gives to trespassers has prompted some state courts to abandon it.

    Answer B is incorrect because the traditional common law treasure trove rule did not discourage finders. To the contrary, the finder received good title. **Answer C is incorrect** because passive owners were penalized, not rewarded, by the common law rule. **Answer D is incorrect** because there is usually no conflict between the common law rule's preference for finders, even trespassers, and the law of adverse possession. Only if a jurisdiction prevents intentional trespassers from gaining title to property by adverse possession is there any tension with the traditional treasure trove rule, but no court has viewed that indirect relationship as a reason for changing the treasure trove rule.

18. **Answer B is the correct answer**. The presence of such a large sum of cash placed in a pail on a shelf suggests that the money was mislaid, not lost or abandoned. Moreover, the failure of anyone to respond to the advertisement indicates that the true owner of the money is unknown. As such, mislaid property belongs to the owner of the land on which it was found.

    Answer A is incorrect because even though the ring was mislaid, the true owner is easily identified, and so the first houseguest will get the ring back. **Answer C is incorrect** because the mere fact that the basketball escaped from the control of its owner does not imply that the ball is abandoned, let alone lost or mislaid. Nor is there a legal rule that entitles a landowner to keep any objects that trespass upon the landowner's land. **Answer D is incorrect** because the possession of any part of an endangered species like a bald eagle is illegal under federal law.

19. **Answer D is the correct answer**. The ring does not qualify as an intervivos gift because Victor never delivered the ring to Mary. Nor will the delivery requirement be excused for such a small item. The ring is not a gift causa mortis, either, because Victor was not in apprehension of imminent death when he promised to give the ring to Mary. Therefore, **Answers A, B, and C are all incorrect**.

20. **Answer D is the correct answer**. Cary obtained voidable title to the copy of *A Connecticut Yankee in King Arthur's Court* when Cary tricked the City Book Store into giving it to him. The store gave Cary the book voluntarily, which creates a voidable title, as opposed to the void title that Cary had to the copy of *Roughing It*. Isabella was a bona fide purchaser of *A Connecticut Yankee in King Arthur's Court*, so she gets to keep it.

    Answer A is incorrect because the mere fact that Conrad's copy of *Roughing It* was stolen does not entitle Conrad to what that book was exchanged for. Conrad will have a cause of action against Cary for theft, and perhaps against the City Book Store who acquired the book from someone who had void title. But Conrad has no rights against Isabella. **Answer B is incorrect** both because he stole *Roughing It* and because he voluntarily surrendered *A Connecticut Yankee in King Arthur's*

Court. **Answer C is incorrect** because the law allows Isabella to keep the book which she acquired as a bona fide purchaser, even though Conrad may be able to get *Roughing It* back from the store.

21. **Answer D is the correct answer**. How Cary acquired the copy of *Roughing It* does not affect the fact that he obtained voidable title to *A Connecticut Yankee in King Arthur's Court* from the City Book Store. Therefore, Isabella obtained that book as a bona fide purchaser just as in Question 20.

    Answer A is incorrect because Conrad does not have any rights against Isabella. **Answer B is incorrect** because Cary voluntarily surrendered *A Connecticut Yankee in King Arthur's Court*. **Answer C is incorrect** because the law allows Isabella to keep the book which she acquired as a bona fide purchaser.

22. **Answer B is the correct answer**. Rancher gets the money if it is viewed as mislaid; Desert Tours gets the money if it is viewed as abandoned. Judges have reached different conclusions in similar cases regarding whether money found in a crashed vehicle is mislaid or abandoned.

    Answers A and D are incorrect because the money was not lost. The fact that the money was in a bag in plain view in the car suggests that the money was not lost, for it would have been easily found if the person who was driving the SUV had cared to look for it. **Answer C is incorrect** because the money did not constitute a treasure trove. According to the law, a treasure trove is defined as property that has been hidden or concealed for so long that it is likely that the true owner is dead or unknown. The seven months that had elapsed since the SUV was stolen from Desert Tours is too short a time to justify the conclusion that the money constitutes a treasure trove.

23. **Answer A is the correct answer**. Intellectual property is a type of personal property, and copyrighted works are a type of personal property.

    Answer B is incorrect because an idea itself is not property. An idea cannot be copyrighted or patented; something more is required to convert the idea into an actual writing or invention before the law recognizes something as property. **Answer C is incorrect** because the law distinguishes crops as real property versus personal property depending upon the status of the crops. Crops like a newly planted vineyard that are still receiving nourishment from the land are regarded as part of the land; crops that are ready for harvest are treated as personal property rather than as part of the land. **Answer D is incorrect** because a building is part of the real property on which it is located.

24. **Answer C is the correct answer**. The marina's acceptance of the boat created a bailment for hire. That bailment could be breached if the marina was negligent. Here, the marina was not negligent because it employed a locked gate to access, and it appears that it was Campisi's loss of the swipe card and his keys that resulted in the loss of the boat.

    Answers A and B are incorrect because there is no evidence that the marina was negligent, let alone grossly negligent. **Answer D is incorrect** because the standard applicable to a bailment for hire is negligence, not gross negligence. The gross negligence would govern if there was a gratuitous bailment, but the reciprocal benefit received by the marina demonstrates that it created a bailment for hire instead.

25.   **Answer A is the correct answer**. Adverse possession provides the greatest obstacle to the original claimants of artwork that was lost or stolen years, or decades, ago. That obstacle has been mitigated by the discovery rule, among other things, in an effort to assure that the original owner and the current possessor are both treated equitably. An international database of lost or stolen works would provide the means by which original owners and interested purchasers can both check to see the status of a particular piece of art.

   Answer B is incorrect because the law of bailments refers to the relationship between the true owner of personal property and an entity that is temporarily entrusted with that property, so the true owner or the original status of that property is irrelevant to their relationship. **Answer C is incorrect** because while an international database of lost or stolen art would help resolve some cases involving finders, it is relatively rare for a finder to discover artwork that is internationally recognized. **Answer D is incorrect** because the characterization of property as a gift or not addresses the status of the property just between the original owner and the putative recipient. The kind of information contained in an international database will not resolve any questions about the intent or delivery of a gift.

26.   **Answer C is the correct answer**. Omar purchased the pen from Samuel the day before Kelly took it from the display case. Unlike a gift, the sale of personal goods does not require their delivery to transfer ownership. Samuel's acceptance of Omar's check created a contract that entitled Omar to the pen.

   Answer A is incorrect because Samuel has accepted Omar's money and provided a written document conveying title to the pen. **Answer B is incorrect** because Samuel did not deliver the pen to Kelly. The fact that Kelly came into possession of the pen does not establish that Samuel delivered it to him. **Answer D is incorrect** because nothing indicates that Jefferson's heirs had an ownership interest in the pen, and Jefferson or his descendants could have conveyed the pen to another party at any time.

27.   **Answer C is the correct answer**. Jeff voluntarily gave the laptop to We Fix It, thus giving the store voidable title to the laptop. Voidable title, in turn, can be conveyed to a good faith purchaser. Monica had no reason to know that the laptop was Jeff's when she bought it from the store, so she qualifies as a good faith purchaser. The fact that she later discovered the mistake does not eliminate that status as a good faith purchaser, either.

   Answers A and B are incorrect because a bona fide purchaser gains better title than the original owner. **Answer D is incorrect** because We Fix It acquired voidable title, not void title, when Jeff voluntarily gave the laptop to the store. The store would have received void title only if it had taken the computer without his knowledge and consent.

28. **Answer C is the correct answer**. This problem is based upon *Basket v. Hassell*, 107 U.S. 602 (1882). Chaney attempted to grant Martin a gift causa mortis. But the death of the donor cannot be a precondition to the validity of a gift causa mortis because such a condition indicates a lack of a present intent to give the gift.

     Answer A is incorrect because the lack of Chaney's present intent to give the certificate of deposit to Martin prevents the transaction from qualifying as a valid gift causa mortis. **Answers B and D are incorrect** because while delivery of the gift was accomplished, the intent to give the certificate was lacking.

29. **Answer B is the correct answer**. Most courts hold that the bank's acceptance of Julia's antique watch created a bailment. The loss of the watch while it was within the bank's control would constitute negligence for which the bank would be liable to Julia.

     Answer A is incorrect because most courts hold that a bailment is not created when landowners allow another person to park a car on their land. An absence of guards or other means of physical control will further support the conclusion that there has not been a bailment. **Answer C is incorrect** because while a bailment was created, a bailor will not be held liable for the loss of very valuable goods that the bailor had no reason to expect where entrusted to its care. **Answer D is incorrect** because there is no indication that the department store took control over the purse, and until it does, no bailment is created.

30. A utilitarian theory emphasizes that the characterization of something as property depends upon whether that property is socially useful. At one time, slavery was regarded as useful by some, but that day has long since passed (at least in the United States). A utilitarian theory also posits that property "is nothing but a basis of expectation," in the words of Jeremy Bentham. Again, the expectation that human slavery is legal has long since disappeared. But a utilitarian struggles to explain to a society that still adheres to slavery why that is impermissible, at least as compared to natural rights, labor, and other leading theories of property.

31. The bank that is now known as First Interstate probably cannot block Suburban Bank from adopting the name First National Bank of Denver. First Interstate has abandoned the trademark that it held in the name "First National Bank of Denver." Abandonment requires a knowing, voluntary relinquishment of a mark. Here First Interstate stated as publicly as it could that the days of its previous name were "behind us." Once the name was abandoned, it reentered the public domain and could be used by the first party to claim it.

32. The California Supreme Court's decision in *Moore v. Regents of the University of California*, 793 P.2d 479 (Cal. 1990), *cert. denied*, 499 U.S. 936 (1991), is the leading case involving the alleged conversion of a patient's body parts that were removed during the course of an operation and later used for medical research. The court explained that there was no conversion because a patient does not expect to retain possession of small body parts that are removed during an operation. Nor was there any precedent for such a conversion claim. The court also explained that a patient's interests were outweighed by the social benefit attending medical research, especially given a patient's admitted right to insist upon informed consent before any parts of his or her body are used in medical research.

33. **Answer D is the correct answer.**

   Wild animals are not owned as property until they are captured. Nancy's photography, even within close proximity, does not demonstrate the reduction to possession that constitutes capture. Therefore, **Answer B is incorrect. Answer A is incorrect** because ownership of the land on which wild animals live does not establish ownership of those animals. **Answer C is incorrect** because even though the state may be said to "own" wild animals within its jurisdiction in some senses, the state does not hold title to wild animals for purposes of conveyancing to another party.

34. **Answer C is the correct answer.** The copyright statute lists "motion pictures" as within the scope of copyright protection. There is no registration requirement for a copyright, so the mere making of the movie will create the copyrighted work.

   Answer A is incorrect because a name is outside the list of things that can be copyrighted. **Answer B is incorrect** because a copyright does not attach until an idea is reduced to writing. Also, a formula is more likely to be patented than copyrighted. **Answer D is not correct** because an oral statement is not copyrighted. Indeed, a copyright is available only to "works of authorship," which the copyright statute defines to include literary works, musical works, dramatic works, pantomimes, choreographic works, pictorial works, graphic works, sculptural works, audiovisual works, sounds recordings, and architectural works — but not simple oral statements.

35. **Answer A is the correct answer**. In the Ninth Circuit case of *Newman v. Sathyavaglswaran*, 287 F.3d 786 (9th Cir. 2002), the court noted that a number of nineteenth century decisions described dead bodies as "quasi property." The case also noted the only other occurrence of that term in the law occurred in *International News Service v. Associated Press*, 248 U.S. 215 (1918), which explained that news was "quasi property."

     Answers B, C, and D are incorrect because no court has described human genes and trade secrets as "quasi property." There is, however, no real legal significance to that term.

36. **Answer D is the correct answer**. Genes are naturally occurring, so they cannot be patented. The fact that the genes are to be used for a different purpose, even such a benevolent one as treating diabetes, does not qualify them for a patent.

     Answer A is incorrect because a hybrid plant can be patented as a new "composition of matter" according to the Patent Act. **Answer (B) is incorrect** because a manufacturing process is a common example of what can be patented. Likewise, **Answer (C) is incorrect** because a machine can be patented. In each instance, the use of the process or the machine does not affect its patentability.

37. **Answer D is the correct answer**. A drawing is copyrighted. As such, it cannot be used without permission for any purpose that does not qualify as fair use. Additionally, the drawing has become the trademark for Thelma's hotels. Again, no one can infringe upon or dilute that trademark without Thelma's permission.

     Answer A is incorrect because a deer is a wild animal that is not owned until it is captured and reduced to possession. The fact that the deer visits the garden every night — or even if the deer lived on Thelma's land — does not constitute possession. **Answer B is incorrect** because Thelma's neighbor owned the deer as a pet, and her neighbor did not lose ownership just because the deer escaped. Thelma's capture of the deer did not give her ownership because the deer was not wild. **Answer C is incorrect** because an animal like the Florida Key deer that is protected by the Endangered Species Act cannot be lawfully possessed.

38. **Answer B is the correct answer**. Article I, section 8, clause 8 of the United States Constitution gives Congress the power to "promote the Progress of Science and useful Arts, by securing for limited Times to Authors and Inventors the exclusive Right to their respective Writings and Discoveries." The provision of property rights is designed to encourage people to create intellectual property even in situations where the constitutional provision does not apply.

Answer A is incorrect because intellectual property rights actually produce monopolies on the protected inventions, writings, and other creations. Those monopolies explain why the Constitution limits the duration of copyrights and patents. **Answer C is incorrect** because copyrights actually protect harmful speech just like beneficial speech, except in the limited circumstances in which the government can regulate speech consistent with the first amendment. **Answer D is incorrect** because the extent of intellectual property rights is unrelated to the extent of real property rights.

39. **Answer A is the correct answer**. This problem is taken from *Mattel, Inc. v. MCA Records, Inc.*, 296 F.3d 894 (9th Cir. 2002), *cert. denied*, 123 S. Ct. 993 (2003). The copyright law *does* apply to live performances. But Mattel does not own a copyright in "Barbie;" it owns a trademark. Aqua is thus potentially liable for trademark infringement, but not copyright infringement.

    Answer B is incorrect because parodies of copyrighted works are permitted, provided that they do not create a likelihood of confusion about the source of the parody. Here the fact that the song does not imply that it was created by Mattel eliminates the likelihood of confusion. **Answer C is incorrect** because it, too, will explain why Mattel will lose: the first amendment does protect a song that is not purely commercial speech. Finally, the song does satisfy the noncommercial use exception which is contained in the Federal Trademark Dilution Act, and thus **Answer D is incorrect.**

40. **Answer C is the correct answer**. To date, and despite numerous proposals and many scholarly suggestions, commercial sperm banks have been subjected to relatively little government regulation. Most states have thus far been unwilling to approve more extensive regulations of such operations. Their unwillingness to do so, however, is unrelated to the other three answers.

    Answer A is incorrect because human body parts are treated as property in a number of instances, though certainly not all of them. **Answer B is incorrect** because the constitutional limits upon state regulation of human reproduction do not prevent all such regulation. A state may regulate when it has a compelling state interest to do so, or perhaps when it assures that the affected parties will not suffer an undue burden. **Answer D is incorrect** because the agreements between commercial sperm banks and donors have been inadequate on a number of instances, yet the appropriate governmental response has yet to be determined.

41. **Answer B is the correct answer**. The fair use provision is a statutory exception to the general provisions of the copyright act that afford writers and other copyright holders a limited monopoly to their works. Fair use recognizes the public's interest in access to written works even while they are protected by copyright law, and the concomitant need to limit the monopoly that the statute grants to copyright holders. The precise scope of the fair use provision remains controversial, especially as technology greatly aids both copyright holders and those desiring to use copyrighted works without having to obtain permission.

    Answer A is incorrect because the nature of ideas as property or not is unrelated to the justifications for the fair use exception. **Answer C is incorrect** because natural rights claims are unlikely to be successful in the context of copyrights, even when asserted by the creators themselves. **Answer D is incorrect** because many commercial works in fact remain valuable for many years or generations, as the recent controversy over the copyrights held by the Walt Disney Company illustrates.

42. Amy will regain title to the land from Babs. Amy's conveyance gave Babs a fee simple determinable while Amy received a possibility of reverter. It is a fee simple determinable because of the durational "so long as" language in the grant. According to the fee simple determinable, Babs will automatically lose her interest in the land if she does not use it as a vacation home during the next 40 years. Amy's possibility of reverter is not subject to the Rule against Perpetuities because it is an interest in the grantor, so that interest is valid. *vested*

43. Chris owns a life estate determinable. The "until" language has a durational aspect which means that the estate will end automatically if Chris graduates from medical school. Sheila has two interests: a reversion that will become possessory once Chris's life estate ends, and a possibility of reverter that will become possessory if Chris graduates from medical school. Neither of Sheila's future interests are subject to the Rule against Perpetuities because they are held by the grantor.

44. Stewart has a fee simple subject to an executory limitation. He retains the townhouse unless or until any of Alice's children reach the age of 30. Larry and Melinda have a springing executory interest in the property subject to partial divestment. It is an executory interest because it was created in a third party; it is springing because it would divest the grantor. Their springing executory interest is subject to the Rule against Perpetuities, but it satisfies the rule using themselves as the lives in being. Larry and Alice will turn 30 or not by the time that each of their lives end. Additionally, Alice cannot have any more children, so Larry's and Melinda's interests are not subject to divestment by any additional siblings. They can, however, partially divest each other, so they would own the townhouse as tenants in common if they both reach the age of 30.

45. Pat's heirs own the farm in fee simple subject to an executory limitation. The devise became effective upon Pat's death in 2001, so Pat's heirs will retain the farm unless or until Pat has any grandchildren born by 2041. Pat's grandchildren own a springing executory interest subject to partial divestment. Their springing executory interest is subject to the Rule against Perpetuities, but it satisfies the rule using Pat's children (John, Jim, and Susan) as the lives in being. Pat cannot have any more children after she dies. John, Jim, and Susan will either have children—who will be Pat's grandchildren—or not by the time that they die. The first of Pat's grandchildren, therefore, will take title to the farm from Pat's heirs, and any additional grandchildren will share in the title to that property.

46. Anne has a life estate. Barbara has a vested remainder subject to a condition subsequent. The remainder is vested because Barbara is ascertained and she gets the property immediately upon the expiration of the preceding estate. Christine has a shifting executory interest. It is shifting because Christine divests a transferee,

not the transferor. That shifting executory interest is valid under the Rule against Perpetuities using either Anne or Barbara as the measuring life.

47. Acme has a reversion by rule because a reversion always exists when an owner transfers less than its entire interest in the property. Isaac has a life estate subject to a condition subsequent, with the commercial use of the property serving as the condition subsequent. The city has a shifting executory interest. That interest is good under the Rule against Perpetuities using Isaac as the measuring life. The commercial restriction lasts as long as the life estate, and after the life estate the property returns to Acme.

48. Gloria has a life estate. Sydney has the reversion that had been created in favor of Julia on March 1, but which Julia then conveyed to Sydney on March 2.

49. Lisa has a reversion by rule because a reversion always exists when an owner transfers less than its entire interest in the property. Irene has a life estate. Brandi has a contingent remainder: it is contingent because it may or may not vest upon the expiration of the preceding estate depending upon how old Brandi is when Irene dies. Brandi's interest satisfies the Rule against Perpetuities using either Irene or Brandi as the measuring life. Likewise, Cherrie has a contingent remainder that is good under the Rule against Perpetuities using either Irene or Brandi as the measuring life.

50. Archibald has a fee simple subject to a condition subsequent. "But if" is not durational language, which explains why Archibald's fee simple is subject to a condition subsequent rather than a fee simple determinable. James has a shifting executory interest that will divest Archibald only if the stated event occurs. James's interest is good under the Rule against Perpetuities using Archibald's children born before Sutton's death as the measuring lives. The class of Archibald's children born before Sutton's death will be closed at the time that Sutton dies. Thus the executory interest will become vested within 21 years of the death of any of Archibald's children—or else it will fail.

51. PLIES has a reversion by rule because a reversion always exists when an owner transfers less than its entire interest in the property. Ken has a life estate. Ken's widow has a contingent remainder for life. It is contingent because Ken's widow is not an ascertained person; he could divorce and remarry someone else who would become his widow upon his death. Ken's widow's interest is good under the Rule against Perpetuities using Ken as the measuring life because Ken's widow will be ascertained when he dies. Ken's widow will take possession immediately upon his death. Marci has a contingent remainder for life. It is contingent because something else must happen before Marci will take possession — namely, the passage of 30 years — rather than treating it as vested even though the passage of 30 years is an event that is sure to occur. Marci's interest is good under the Rule against Perpetuities using Marci as the measuring life.

52. **Answer B is the correct answer**. The children of Andrew have a contingent remainder for life. It is a remainder because it is capable of being possessory

immediately upon the termination of the preceding estate. It is contingent because those children are not yet ascertained. That interest satisfies the Rule against Perpetuities using Andrew as the measuring life because Andrew's children will be ascertained when Andrew dies.

Answer A is incorrect because the number of children that Andrew will have was not ascertained when Sheila died. **Answer C is incorrect** because Kerry's interest becomes possessory upon the expiration of the preceding estate, rather than waiting for the occurrence of a particular event that would create an executory interest. **Answer D is incorrect** because Kerry's contingent remainder satisfied the Rule against Perpetuities using Andrew as the measuring life.

53. **Answer C is the correct answer.** Alexandra's siblings have a contingent remainder. Bertrand's interest is subject to open because Alexandra's parents might have more children. It is contingent because a conveyance to a class becomes vested for each member of the class only once it is vested for every member of the class.

A contingent remainder is subject to the Rule against Perpetuities, so **Answer A is incorrect. Answer B is incorrect** because Alexandra may or may not die more than 21 years before her parents have additional children who would be part of the class holding the contingent remainder. Thus, Alexandra cannot serve as the measuring life to determine the validity of her siblings' interest under the Rule. But Alexandra's parents can serve as the measuring life, so **Answer C is correct.** Her parents are ascertainable, and when they die, we will know then who Alexandra's siblings are. **Answer D is incorrect** because the possibility that Alexandra's parents will have additional children ends when her parents die, which is when Alexandra's siblings become ascertainable and their interest vests.

54. **Answer D is the correct answer.** Stuart's lineal descendants alive in 2010 have a contingent remainder. It is contingent because those descendants were not ascertainable at the time of William's death. Their interest is good under the Rule against Perpetuities because we will know in less than 21 years which of Stuart's lineal descendants are alive on January 1, 2010. You can use *anyone* who was alive when William died — literally — as a measuring life and just add 21 years.

Answers A, B, and C are all incorrect because they describe people who are alive at the time of the devise. But no one who is born after the devise can serve as a life in being at the time of the devise for purposes of the Rule, so **Answer D is correct.**

55. **Answer A is the correct answer.** Cooper's heirs own a life estate per autre vie — a life estate for the duration of Andrew's life. Cooper obtained Andrew's life estate, so it passed to Cooper's heirs upon his death.

Answer B is incorrect because Andrew's conveyance remains valid despite Cooper's death. **Answer C is incorrect** because Beatrice owns a vested remainder that will not become possessory until Andrew dies. **Answer D is incorrect** because Acme's conveyance remains valid despite Cooper's death as well.

56. **Answer A is the correct answer.**

Angela's will gave Jackson's daughters a remainder, not an executory interest, because that interest will become possessory immediately upon the termination of the preceding estate, so **Answer D is incorrect**. The remainder is contingent because the class of Jackson's daughters is not ascertainable yet, so **Answer B is incorrect**. But that contingent remainder is void under the Rule against Perpetuities, so **Answer C is incorrect**. It is possible that a daughter of Jackson who has yet to be born will become a medical doctor more than 21 years after the death of Jackson or Jackson's daughter Jenny. Angela's heirs have a reversion which will thus become possessory upon the end of Jackson's life estate.

57. **Answer A is the correct answer**. A fee tail was one of several medieval devices to keep land in the family, and thus restrict the alienability of property.

   Answer C is incorrect because, as stated above, a fee tail was designed to keep land within the same family for several generations. **Answer B is incorrect** as well because it describes the manner in which a fee tail could be created. **Answer D is incorrect** because life estates are now used to control inheritance, and thus they are the property interests most likely to replace the functioning of a fee tail.

58. **Answer B is the correct answer**. The "with the understanding" language has no legal effect, so Luke holds the property in fee simple absolute regardless of how the property is used.

   Answer A is incorrect because Luke received a fee simple determinable that will revert to Lauer's automatically if Luke does not use the land for a grocery store. **Answer C is incorrect** because Luke received Greenacre in fee simple subject to a condition subsequent. That estate will not terminate automatically if Luke does not use the land for a grocery store, but the fact that the exercise of the right of entry can divest Luke shows that Luke does not own the land in fee simple absolute. **Answer D is incorrect,** too. Luke conveyed a fee simple determinable to Lauer's. That estate will end automatically if Luke fails to operate his grocery store there, and the fee simple title to the property will revert back to Luke. Luke will continue to hold his life estate determinable assuming that his sporting goods store sells tennis balls, but that is irrelevant once Luke regains the fee simple title upon the expiration of the fee simple determinable that had been held by Lauer's.

59. **Answer C is the correct answer**. Cathy conveyed a fee simple determinable for the historical society with a shifting executory interest to Joyce. That executory interest is valid under the Rule against Perpetuities because it must vest or fail within 20 years, which will be within 21 years of the life of anyone in being at the time of the conveyance.

   Answer A is incorrect because Joyce owns the lake house in fee simple subject to an executory limitation. **Answer B is incorrect** because Joyce owns a vested remainder in the ranch that will become possessory when Cathy dies. **Answer D is incorrect** because Joyce has no interest in the lot. Cathy is still alive, so the fact that her will would give Joyce an interest in the lot means nothing because Cathy can change her will at any time before she dies.

60. **Answer B is the correct answer**. The conveyance from Axle gave Lucy a life estate and Annie a vested remainder. That remainder was vested because Lucy's "eldest daughter" was ascertainable as Annie at the time of the conveyance from Axle. Upon Lucy's death, Annie's remainder became possessory. But Annie had conveyed that remainder to the Prairie Land Trust, which now holds the land in fee simple.

    Answer A is incorrect because Axle did not retain any property interest once it conveyed the riverfront property. **Answer C is incorrect** because Tanya was not Lucy's "eldest daughter." It is possible that "her eldest daughter" could be interpreted to mean the oldest daughter of Lucy's who was living at the time of Lucy's death, but the better interpretation construes "her eldest daughter" at the time of the conveyance. **Answer D is incorrect** because Lucy could not convey a greater interest in the property than she owned herself. Dean Walter thus entered into the five-year lease with the risk that Lucy would not live five more years, and thus her interest in the land would end.

61. **Answer B is the correct answer**. Jane's attempt to convey a tenancy by the entirety to Julie and Henry failed because you cannot own property in a tenancy by the entirety if you are not married. An unsuccessful effort to create a tenancy by the entirety will either result in a joint tenancy or a tenancy in common, with different jurisdictions reaching different conclusions.

    The fact that Julie and Henry got married two years later does not change the status of the estate that Jane conveyed — and thus **Answer A is incorrect**. **Answer C is incorrect** because Jane gave Julie an executory interest if she and Henry ever got divorced, not a contingent remainder. **Answer D is incorrect** since that executory interest is shifting, not springing, because it would divest a transferee instead of Jane. The shifting executory interest satisfies the Rule against Perpetuities using either Julie or Henry as the measuring life.

62. **Answer A is the correct answer**. Mountain Realty conveyed a life estate to Elaine while keeping the reversion for itself. Regardless of how Elaine conveyed her interest, the property was always destined to return to Mountain Realty upon her death.

    Answer B is incorrect both because Elaine was incapable of devising her life estate in the ten acres of land, and even if she had been allowed to do so, Randy attempted to convey his interest to Sara. **Answer C is incorrect** because she obtained the land from Randy, who did not own any interest that he could convey. **Answer D is incorrect** because the county did obtain the ten acres from Elaine in fee simple, but only for the duration of Elaine's life. When Elaine died, her life estate ended, and the county's interest in the land ended, too.

63. **Answer D is the correct answer**. Gerald's will does not state an explicit condition upon Carla's ownership of the home. The "for her home" language is most likely to be viewed as without legal effect because it merely describes Gerald's plan for the home rather than indicating that Carla will lose the property if she no longer uses it as her home. Accordingly, Carla received the home in fee simple absolute, and Mark did not receive a property interest in the home.

Answers A, B, and C are incorrect because the devise did not create any future interests. If Gerald's will had stated instead that the home was devised to Carla "provided that she used it as her home, then to Carla's children," then Mark (along with Thomas and Carla's other children) would have owned a shifting executory interest as indicated in Answer (C). Or if the will had stated that the home was devised to Carla "for her life, then to Carla's children," then Mark would have held a vested remainder subject to opening as indicated in Answer (A). That remainder would be vested because it would have become possessory immediately upon the termination of the preceding estate, and it would be subject to open if Carla had any more children besides Mark and Thomas.

64. New Campbell follows the common law rules for the distribution of property upon divorce. Accordingly, Beth and Donald are entitled to an equitable distribution of their property. The rights established by the IFQ are valuable and readily quantifiable, so unlike more speculative items such as contingency fee agreements, they constitute property for purposes of equitable distribution. Donald already held such rights when he got married to Beth, but the value of those rights increased by one million dollars from $800,000 at the time they were married in 1993 to $1,800,000 in 2003. Donald kept acquiring those rights as a result of the labor that he exerted fishing while he was married to Beth, which gives Beth a right to share in at least the additional $1,000,000 of the IFQ rights. Beth is thus entitled to an equitable share of all of their marital property, including the $1,000,000 in additional value of the IFQ rights that were gained during their marriage.

65. George owns the house in fee simple. George and Sylvia still owned the house as tenants by the entirety until Sylvia died. A tenancy by the entirety includes a right of survivorship, which means that all of the property goes to the surviving tenant upon the death of the other tenant. The interest held by a tenancy by the entirety cannot be devised, so Sylvia's will could not transfer her interest in the house to Betsy. Nor did Sylvia's stated intent to sell the property affect the property rights because no action was ever taken to realize that desire, and a tenancy by the entirety can only be terminated by death or divorce. Thus, Sylvia's property interest ended with her death, and George obtained all of the property.

66. Gloria owns a two-thirds interest in the ten acres and Doris owns a one-third interest. That occurred as follows: When Alex conveyed his property to his wife Doris in 1959, he destroyed the joint tenancy by severing the unity of time. As a result, in 1959 Bobby and Carlos owned two-thirds as joint tenants between themselves, and Doris owned one-third of the land as a tenant in common. When Bobby died in 1959, his interest in the land automatically shifted to Carlos by the right of survivorship, so Carlos then owned a two-thirds interest in the land. Next, upon the death of Carlos, his two-thirds interest was devised to Gloria. Eduardo did not own an interest in the property, so his death did not affect the property.

67. **Answer D is the correct answer**. Slightly more than half community property states mandate an equal distribution of marital assets, not an equitable distribution. The mutual fund containing the savings from their income is a marital asset because Melinda and Brandon acquired it while they were married. By contrast, the car was a gift to Brandon alone, and such individualized gifts are treated as separate property, not marital property.

Answer A is incorrect both because Melinda is not entitled to the car and because a minority of community property states require an equitable distribution of marital property. **Answer B is incorrect** because Melinda is most likely entitled to an equal distribution, or perhaps an equitable distribution, of the mutual fund. **Answer C is incorrect** because Melinda is not entitled to any part of the value of the car.

68. **Answer D is the correct answer.** Gerald's conveyance of his interest in the vacation home did not terminate the tenancy by the entirety because only mutual consent, death, or divorce can do that. Gerald was free, however, to convey his interest in the land, but it retained its status as a tenancy by the entirety with Alice. Upon Gerald's death, Alice took the whole property by operation of the right of survivorship inherent in the tenancy by the entirety. Gerald's creditors, by contrast, got nothing. They would have obtained the whole property, though, if Alice had died before Gerald. That did not happen, though, so **Answers A, B, and C are all incorrect** because they wrongly indicate that Gerald's creditors have a property interest in the vacation home.

69. **Answer B is the correct answer.** A partition action is available whenever two or more tenants in common are unable to agree about the appropriate use, or disposition, of their property. The fact that Joseph has lived there since before Kelly obtained an interest in the property will not allow Joseph to defeat Kelly's legitimate interests as a tenant in common.

    Answer A is incorrect because tenants in common hold equal rights, regardless of whether they are in possession of the property or not. **Answer C is incorrect** because a tenancy in common can be conveyed without destroying the interest, so Joseph did not obtain the land in fee when Frank sold it. **Answer D is incorrect** because Joseph cannot block a partition action simply by paying rent to Kelly. Joseph may persuade Kelly not to seek a partition, or Kelly may be entitled to rent in limited circumstances, but Kelly will always retain the right to seek a partition sale of the house if he chooses to do so.

70. **Answer D is the correct answer.** A joint tenancy requires four unities — of time, title, interest, and possession — and the destruction of any of them destroys the joint tenancy. Harry's sale of the house will destroy the joint tenancy and produce a tenancy in common instead.

    Answer A is incorrect because a marital separation does not eliminate any of the four unities. Likewise, the fact that Harry and Winona have children does not automatically give those children a property interest in the home or otherwise destroy any of the unities. Thus, **Answer B is incorrect. Answer C is incorrect** because most jurisdictions — though not all — hold that a mortgage functions simply as a contract and not as a property interest, so it fails to destroy any of the unities.

71. **Answer C is the correct answer.** A dower gave a wife an interest in her deceased husband's property for the rest of her life, but she could not devise that interest upon her death.

    The wife would not get the property in fee simple, so **Answer A is incorrect.** Nor would she get the property as a fee simple determinable, for it was her death that would terminate her property rights, so **Answer B is incorrect. Answer D is also incorrect** because a dower did yield a real property interest, albeit a limited one.

72. **Answer B is the correct answer**. Eric's income will be viewed as property owned by both him and Anita because he earned it while they were married.

    Eric's law degree, by contrast, was granted before they were married, so Anita has no claim to it, and **Answer A is incorrect**. **Answer C is also incorrect** because most jurisdictions hold that contingency fee agreements are too speculative to qualify as a current property interest. **Answer D is incorrect** because the yacht was a gift specifically to Eric, and thus it is separate property outside of the marital estate.

73. **Answer B is the correct answer**. The destruction of the home — even to replace it with a nicer, larger home — cannot be done unilaterally by one co-tenant. Jim will either have to obtain John's consent or seek a partition of their respective interests in the property.

    Answer A is incorrect because a tenant who is actually present on the premises is authorized to consent to a search of at least the common areas of the cottage. Whether or not Jim could consent to a police search of John's bedroom within the cottage is a more difficult question, but it is not the question here. **Answer C is incorrect** because any co-tenant can obtain a mortgage, albeit only on their share of the property. Likewise, **Answer D is incorrect** because a co-tenant can convey his or her interest to someone else. The couple would have the right to retire in the cottage while John is still living there, but whether they would want to do so does not affect Jim's ability to convey his interest to them.

74. **Answer B is the correct answer**. This problem is loosely based upon *Tackett v. State*, 2003 Tex. App. LEXIS 3760 (Tex. Ct. App. May 1, 2003). Presumably Anita and Greg owned the pickup truck as tenants in common, for that is the default rule for concurrent owners. Even if they owned it as joint tenants, though, the answer is the same. The destruction of property by one of its owners without the consent of the other owners constitutes waste.

    Answer A is incorrect because Anita and Greg jointly owned the truck, probably as tenants in common, though the precise nature of their ownership rights is unimportant here. **Answer C is incorrect** because the truck would constitute marital property that is subject to distribution upon their divorce, so Anita could not destroy that property. **Answer D is incorrect** because the general right to destroy one's property does not apply to property that is owned by more than one person.

75. **Answer D is the correct answer**. Sebastian and Cheryl purchased the property separately, not as concurrent owners. Both parcels will be subject to the appropriate distribution if Sebastian and Cheryl get divorced, but there is no indication of that occurring here. Title to the property remains with the party who purchased it from Alma. By contrast, **Answers A, B, and C are each incorrect** because they wrongly presume that Sebastian and Cheryl acquired the property together.

76. The advantages include the absence of FHA's exceptions for housing sold or rented by the owner and residential dwellings in which the owner lives. The primary disadvantage is that section 1982 only applies to racial discrimination, and not to other kinds of discrimination. Section 1982 also requires proof of a discriminatory intent. And section 1982 does not apply to discriminatory advertisements for housing that indicate that only people of a certain race, gender, or religion are welcome to apply.

77. The illegal lease doctrine has not been adopted in other jurisdictions because of its limited application and because of the availability of better solutions to the problem of affordable housing. The doctrine only applies to housing code violations that existed in rental housing at the time the parties agreed to the lease. As such, the doctrine does not provide any remedy for housing code violations or other problems that develop after the tenant signs the lease. Nor does the doctrine address minor and technical housing code violations or to violations that were actually and constructively unknown to the landlord. Meanwhile, warranties of habitability have evolved to provide a more effective remedy to inadequate rental housing regardless of the time when a problem arises. Also, in some jurisdictions the government has become more effective in investigating and punishing housing code violations, which avoids the additional difficulty of tenants who are unaware of their rights.

78. Courts are divided concerning the duty of a landlord to control the actions of some of their tenants that bother other of their tenants. In many instances, a court will hold that a landlord does not have a duty to act to abate a nuisance or a crime committed by a tenant. If a court does find such a duty, then a failure to act could breach the covenant of quiet enjoyment and result in a constructive eviction. A tenant who has been constructively evicted may sue the landlord for damages, and perhaps the tenant will be able to leave the premises and stop paying rent, although that latter option is not available in many jurisdictions. A tenant would want to claim that a landlord's failure to control the actions of another tenant constitutes a breach of the warranty of habitability, for such a breach offers the tenant a wider variety of remedies, including staying on the premises while refusing to pay rent, suing for compensatory damages, or even suing for punitive damages. But courts will be reluctant to view a landlord's failure to act in response to a complaint about another tenant as a breach of the warranty of habitability.

79. Supporters of rent control advance a number of common arguments. First, they insist that housing is more worthy of government protection than other commodities because housing is an essential human right, and because housing is so personal to its occupant. Rent controls make housing affordable and thus are able to serve these important societal purposes. Second, the existing housing market is not

sufficiently competitive. There is not enough housing, especially housing that is affordable to those with low incomes, so government intervention is necessary to achieve the appropriate price that would not be reached by simple reliance upon supply and demand. Third, the government should act to maintain existing communities that would otherwise be disrupted by the displacement of residents who can no longer afford to live there. In other words, even if affordable housing can be found in a nearby neighborhood, the constant flux of people moving from one home to another prevents the creation and maintenance of stable communities that provide numerous benefits to society as a whole.

80. A tenant asking a court to recognize an implied warranty of habitability may advance a number of arguments. First, many courts have already found such a warranty, and those decisions provide persuasive precedents for a court considering the question now. Second, an implied warranty of habitability is more consistent with the realities of modern urban living than the older real property theories that denied such a warranty. Likewise, an implied warranty is consistent with contemporary contract principles that are informing the development of landlord/tenant law. Finally, judicial recognition of an implied warranty furthers the important public policy of assuring that everyone is able to live in adequate housing.

81. **Answer C is the correct answer**. Rent control laws are consistent with federal and state constitutional provisions only if the laws guarantee landlords a reasonable amount of rents. While there is no bright-line test for the precise return to which a landlord is entitled, an ordinance limiting a landlord's rent increases to 50% of the annual inflation rate is undoubtedly the most constitutionally problematic of any of the ordinances listed here.

     Answer A is incorrect because rent control ordinances have been commonly upheld absent a war, notwithstanding the original emergency rationale for the constitutionality of rent controls. **Answer B is incorrect** because it simply describes the cash flow method of determining the return to which a landlord is entitled. The cash flow method is one of several methods that courts have upheld in judging the minimum return to which a landlord is entitled. **Answer D is incorrect** because rent control ordinances usually contain such succession provisions, and they have not only upheld them, but courts have extended them to broader understandings of "family members," too.

82. **Answer D is the correct answer**. In most jurisdictions, the implied warranty of habitability does not extend to commercial properties.

     Answer A is incorrect because most jurisdictions do not allow the implied warranty of habitability to be waived by the parties. **Answer B is incorrect** because the warranty governs the condition of the premises regardless of when a problem occurred. **Answer C is incorrect** because the warranty guarantees the condition of the premises, not just a landlord's effort to solve any problems. The warranty does not apply to problems that are de minimis, but that is unrelated to whether or not the landlord was able to remedy them.

83. **Answer B is the correct answer**. A periodic tenancy is a leasehold estate that lasts for a period of a specified duration and then continues for succeeding periods

until either the landlord or the tenant gives notice of termination. As such, a landlord may terminate a periodic tenancy for any reason, or for no reason. That, at least, was the rule in Utah until the enactment of the Mobile Home Park Residency Act, which prohibited a landlord from terminating a lease without cause.

A term of years, on the other hand, is a leasehold estate that lasts for a fixed period of time or for a period of time that can be calculated with a beginning and ending date. The automatic expiration of a term of years means that a landlord need not act to terminate the lease. Thus, **Answers A and C are incorrect. Answer D is incorrect** because the statute modifies a periodic tenancy (Answer (B)).

84. **Answer D is the correct answer**. While the English rule implies a covenant for the landlord to put a tenant in actual possession of property that the tenant has leased, the American rule does not imply any such covenant or duty. The American rule posits that landlords and tenants are equally on notice that this could become a potential problem, and equally capable of resolving it. Moreover, tenants can protect themselves by requesting an express covenant if they are concerned that someone else may be occupying the premises. Under the American rule, then, a landlord does not have a duty to ensure that a trespasser like John Crosby is removed from the leased property, so **Answer D is correct**.

On the other hand, the landlord does have a duty not to interfere with the tenant's possession, so **Answer A is incorrect.** The landlord's duty extends to someone who is there with the landlord's permission, so **Answer B is incorrect**. And the landlord has the duty to make sure that no one else claims title to the land, such as Bob Clauss, so **Answer C is incorrect**.

85. **Answer A is the correct answer**. A breach of an implied warranty of habitability is the most likely instance in which a tenant can leave her leased premises without having to pay further rent or otherwise honor the terms of the lease. While there are several alternative tests for determining what constitutes a breach, the basic premise of the warranty is that a landlord has a duty to ensure that the leased premises satisfy elementary standards of habitability. A failure to provide running water to an apartment for six weeks will satisfy that standard, so Linus will breach the warranty despite his efforts to remedy the problem.

Answer B is incorrect because a single, brief problem will not entitle a tenant to abandon the premises and avoid any further duties under the breach. **Answer C is incorrect** because it is doubtful that a landlord has a duty to Twyla to control the activity — even the crimes — of other tenants. **Answer D is incorrect** because few states have extended an implied warranty of habitability to commercial premises such as Tori's store.

86. **Answer C is the correct answer**. An estate at will exists when a lease is for an unspecified period that lasts as long as both the landlord and the tenant desire. Only notice is required for termination of the estate.

Answer A is incorrect because an estate of years lasts for a fixed time period or for a period of time that can be calculated with a beginning and ending date.

The estate ends upon the expiration of the specified term or the stated event or condition. **Answer B is incorrect** because a periodic estate lasts for a fixed period that continues for succeeding periods until either the landlord or the tenant gives notice of termination. **Answer D is incorrect** because an estate at sufferance arises when a tenant holds over after the termination of the estate. An estate at sufferance establishes a new estate that lasts for the period of the rent or as an estate at will.

86. **Answer B is the correct answer**. Answer (B) is correct because most jurisdictions will describe it as a partial assignment instead of as a sublease. A partial assignment occurs when a tenant conveys all of his or her interest in part of the leased premises. Julia's conveyance of one of her two acres, therefore, established a partial assignment.

    Answer A is incorrect because it describes an assignment. Unlike a sublease, an assignment occurs when a tenant conveys all of his or her interest in the leased premises, as Julia has done in Answer A. **Answer C is incorrect** because a sublease occurs when a tenant conveys part of his or her interest in the leased premised. When Julia rents the two acres to Franklin for seven of the nine years remaining on her lease, that constitutes a sublease. **Answer D is incorrect** because it lasts for less than the entire duration held by Julia, so it describes a sublease instead of a partial assignment.

88. **Answer A is the correct answer**. A term of years ends automatically upon the expiration of the duration stated in the lease, so Susan will be able to leave without informing her landlord beforehand.

    Answers B and C are incorrect because notice is required before either a periodic tenancy or a tenancy at will are terminated. Thus, for the same reason, **Answer D is incorrect** as well.

89. **Answer A is the correct answer**. A tenant such as Thelma is responsible for evicting trespassers once she actually takes possession. Francis was a trespasser, so it was Thelma's duty to remove her, not Lance's. Thelma thus has no excuse for not paying the rent that she owed to Lance.

    Answer B is incorrect because Francis has not entered into a lease or any other agreement that obligates her to pay Lance (or, for that matter, Thelma) for the estate. **Answers C and D are incorrect** because there was no interference with Thelma's premises when Lance delivered them to her in 1995. Francis arrived five years later, so any duty to deliver the premises had long since been satisfied, regardless of whether the American or English rule for the delivery of possession applied.

90. **Answer D is the correct answer**. The federal Fair Housing Act, 42 U.S.C. §§ 3601-3619, 3631, prohibits discrimination "against any person in the terms, conditions or privileges of rental or a dwelling because of a handicap of that renter." Discrimination is defined as "a refusal to make reasonable accommodations in rules, policies, practices, or services, when such accommodations may be necessary to

afford such person equal opportunity to use and enjoy a dwelling." Lois's refusal to allow a deaf tenant to install a special telephone line at his own expense constitutes a failure to make "a reasonable accommodation" that "may be necessary to afford such person equal opportunity to use and enjoy a dwelling."

Answer A is incorrect because Lois obtained a court order that entitled her to evict Tom from the premises. With such an order, courts have held that a landlord owes no duty of care for an evicted tenant's property. **Answer B is incorrect** because Lou was renting commercial premises. While many states prohibit a landlord from exercising self-help to regain control of its premises, some states refuse to extend the rule against self-help to commercial lease because of the greater importance of your residence, the need for replacement commercial space is less vital, and the equality of bargaining power in commercial leases. **Answer C is incorrect** because a landlord is free to refuse to renew a lease provided that the reason is not one of the few listed in federal, state, or local anti-discrimination laws. Dislike of a tenant's friends is not protected under those laws.

91. **Answer D is correct** because a periodic tenancy can be terminated only upon sufficient notice. The length of the required notice varies between jurisdictions, but no state allows termination upon just one day's notice.

Answers A, B, and C are each incorrect because the landlords will be able to terminate the leases as they desire. **Answer A is incorrect** because Teresa agreed to the termination of the lease. Larry could not terminate the lease unilaterally because it had not yet expired, but the parties are always free to agree to end the lease if they both agree. **Answer B is incorrect** because the four-year lease was a term of years that ended automatically once the four years elapsed. Twyla could have stayed longer as a holdover tenant if Louis agreed, but Louis was authorized to treat Twyla as a trespasser instead if she stayed on the premises after the lease ended. **Answer C is incorrect** because a landlord — and usually a tenant, too — can terminate a tenancy at will at any time upon notice.

92. **Answer C is the correct answer**. Most jurisdictions forbid the parties to a lease from waiving an implied warranty of habitability. With that warranty in place, the lack of security presented by the inability to lock the front door should qualify to render the premises uninhabitable, so Sonja can leave the premises and stop paying rent.

Answer A is incorrect because the home would probably not be deemed uninhabitable if locked doors are not an essential feature of living in the community. Habitability is judged in part by where a tenant lives — air condition is not essential in Minnesota, while heat might not be essential in southern Florida. The need for locked doors could depend upon the neighborhood as well. **Answer B is incorrect** because a landlord must be notified of the problem with the premises before a tenant can declare them uninhabitable and move out. **Answer D is incorrect** because the landlord is not responsible for Sonja's failed improvements, so the landlord has not breached a duty that would enable Sonja to leave the premises and stop paying rent.

93. **Answer D is the correct answer**. A landlord cannot easily pass along the costs of compliance with the housing code to the tenants that benefit from the improved

housing. Thus Judge Posner, for example, insists that the enforcement of housing codes leads to a substantial reduction in the supply of low income housing and a substantial rise in the price of the remaining supply. Of course, proponents of housing code enforcement contest these claims, but they are a standard part of the debate about the best means of securing affordable and adequate housing.

Answer A is incorrect because most housing codes are anything but vague. To the contrary, housing codes are incredibly detailed. **Answer B is incorrect** because nearly every jurisdiction has enacted a housing code, though enforcement of those codes varies widely between jurisdictions. **Answer C is incorrect** because courts have been quite willing to refashion landlord/tenant law in recent decades, with particular attention paid to the relative rights of landlords and tenants. The sudden ubiquity of an implied warranty of habitability is just one illustration of judicial willingness to modify landlord/tenant law to respond to contemporary needs.

94. **Answer B is the correct answer.** In 1988, Congress amended the Fair Housing Act to prohibit discrimination based on "familial status." The legislative history of that provision indicates that Congress wanted to eliminate discrimination against families with children. A landlord that refuses to rent to an apartment to Tom because he is "the father of six children" has probably violated the FHA.

     Answer A is incorrect because the FHA does not prohibit landlords from making decisions based upon sexual orientation. A number of state and local laws prohibit such actions, but efforts to add sexual orientation to the coverage of the FHA have failed. **Answer C is incorrect** because a landlord's decision based upon a tenant's reputation is not within the scope of the FHA, at least so long as the reputation itself is not linked to a protected characteristic. **Answer D is incorrect** because occupation is not one of the protected characteristics covered by the FHA.

95. **Answer C is the correct answer.** The RAA entered into a sublease with the law firm — the term of the lease between the RAA and the law firm was less than the RAA's remaining interest in its lease with URP. Because it was a sublease, the RAA retained the duty to pay the rent to URP. The law firm's subsequent breach of its duty to pay rent to the RAA does not affect the RAA's distinct duty to pay rent to URP.

     Answer A is incorrect because a tenancy at will may be terminated at any time by either party. **Answer B is incorrect** because the government's acquisition of property by eminent domain terminates the tenant's obligation to pay rent. **Answer D is incorrect** because the doctrine of frustration of purpose authorizes a tenant to terminate a lease when the intended use is known to the landlord, that use is completely frustrated, and the event causing the frustration of that use was unforeseeable.

96. **Answer D is the correct answer.** The lease created a periodic tenancy. That tenancy lasts for an indefinite duration until it is terminated upon adequate notice by one of the parties. If Sandy and Greg provided adequate notice, then the tenancy is ended and Suarez will not be able to recover any rent from Sandy and Greg.

Answers A and B are incorrect because Suarez cannot insist that Sandy and Greg stay in the house, for a periodic tenancy can be terminated by the tenants at any time upon adequate notice. Moreover, nothing in the lease's provisions obligate Sandy and Greg to live in the house, which is another reason why **Answer B is incorrect**. **Answer C is incorrect** because the courts will employ their equitable powers to fashion an appropriate remedy for the breach of a lease if the lease itself fails to specify a remedy.

97. **Answer C is the correct answer**. Some states, cities, and other local governments have included marital status within the scope of their prohibitions against housing discrimination. Other localities do not list marital status as a prohibited basis for a landlord's decision. Accordingly, the legality of Lois's action will most likely depend upon the jurisdiction in which she lives.

    Answer A is incorrect because while the constitutionality of RLUIPA could affect Lois's ability to exclude Tom and Doris, the likelihood of that statute disposing of this case but for a holding that the statute is unconstitutional is decidedly less likely than Answer (D). **Answer B is incorrect** because the scope of the Fair Housing Act has not been interpreted to extend rights to unmarried couples, although the Act's prohibition against discrimination based upon "familial status" could conceivably apply. Moreover, the Fair Housing Act does not apply to the decisions of landowners who rent out a room in the house in which they are living, regardless of the reason for such decisions. **Answer D is incorrect** because traditionally the common law provided few restrictions upon a landlord's ability to exclude unwanted tenants.

98.   Justin owns the property. The recording statutes protect the claims of those who obtain title to property and record that deed so that their title is publicly known. But only those who give value for a deed are entitled to rely on the protections of the recording system. Justin's deed is still valid because he obtained the property from Stella, who did in fact own the property. Justin would lose to any subsequent purchaser for value if Stella sold the property again after she sold it to Justin. Quincy, however, received the ten acres of land as gift, and his failure to pay value for the land precludes him from relying upon the recording statute. Justin thus prevails against Quincy as the first party to acquire title from Stella.

99.   The Jacksons own the new land. The Madisons owned that land in 1977, at the end of the fifteen years when the course of the river was changing. The gradual, imperceptible addition of the land constituted accretion, and the law gives the owner of the riparian land the title to the land added by accretion. The Madisons thus owned the land in 1977. But the Jacksons used that land for their cattle from 1962 until 1977. Their use qualifies as adverse possession: the fence indicated that it was under a claim of right, their use was exclusive, it was open and visible for anyone to see, and it was for the statutory period. Thus title to the new land had already shifted to the Jacksons by the time the Madisons returned there in 1990.

100. Madison probably owns the property. To be effective, a deed must intend to transfer title to property, it must be delivered with the intent that it be presently operative, and it must be accepted. Delivery does not necessarily involve the physical transfer of the deed. Delivery may be presumed if the grantee possesses the deed, the deed has been recorded, or the deed has been acknowledged. On the other hand, a presumption that delivery has not occurred arises if the grantor still has the deed. Here delivery did not occur in 1987 when Jim attempted to sell his country estate to Dawn, for Jackson retained possession of the deed. Nor is there any indication that Dawn accepted the deed before 1987, either. In 1998, though, Dawn obtained the deed, albeit unknowingly, and she apparently accepted it. By that time, Jim had already sold the property to Madison four years before. Madison will argue that the conveyance to Dawn failed for lack of delivery and acceptance, or alternatively, laches bars Dawn from contesting Madison's title. Madison's arguments will likely succeed, though the law is not certain. Note also that Madison has not been on the property long enough to establish adverse possession.

101. There are three theories that explain why airplanes are not serial trespassers. First, aircraft are treated as an exception to the ordinary rule of ad coelum, which entitles landowners to the airspace above their property. Second, the airspace that a landowner owns pursuant to the ad coelum is limited to a certain height above the land so that airplanes flying above that height are not within anyone's property. Third,

the ad coelum doctrine is rejected, but landowners are given a dormant right to build into the airspace above their land, albeit not so high as to interfere with aviation.

102.   Washington is the sovereign authority over the additional 24.5 acres of the island. The facts in this question are essentially the same as the dispute concerning Ellis Island that the Supreme Court confronted in *New Jersey v. New York*, 523 U.S. 767 (1998). There the Court explained that the common law treats the fill placed by the federal government as avulsion. It is avulsion because its presence was immediately obvious, not the gradual and imperceptible additions to land that qualify as accretion. Avulsion does not affect the boundary between the states, so the hypothetical Wanapam Island is under the jurisdiction of Washington because of its presence on Washington's side of the boundary between the states.

103.   **Answer C is the correct answer**. Celia is a mistaken improver. She did not intentionally trespass in order to obtain the grapes. She then transformed the grapes into something far more valuable. That transformation caused the original grapes to become a different species, so Celia will be able to keep everything except that she will have to reimburse her neighbor for the original value of the grapes.

       Answer A is incorrect because the meteorite that Anna took belonged to her neighbor by virtue of the ownership of the land on which it fell, and Anna was an intentional trespasser onto her neighbor's land. **Answer B is incorrect** because Betty was an intentional trespasser and thus outside the rules protecting "mistaken" improvers. **Answer D is incorrect** because Daphne worked only an insignificant improvement in the value of the turtle shell, so her neighbor will be entitled to get it back.

104.   **Answer B is the correct answer**. The owner of the surface estate is entitled to use reasonable means to take the natural gas that lies beneath its land, even if the drilling takes gas that has migrated from its original position beneath land owned by someone else.

       By contrast, states have different rules for groundwater: the absolute ownership doctrine allows landowners to withdraw an unlimited amount of water from beneath the land that they own, but the correlative rights doctrine limits landowners to a reasonable share of the groundwater based upon the proportion of the land that they own. **Answer A is thus incorrect** because there are many state that follow the correlative rights doctrine that prevents landowners from taking exclusive possession of all of the water beneath their property. Likewise, **Answer D is incorrect** because the relics will either be owned by the owner of the land immediately above where they were discovered, or by the tribe or by the tribal descendants pursuant to the Native American Graves Protection and Repatriation Act. **Answer (C) is incorrect** because each part of a cave belongs to the owner of the land immediately above it.

105.   **Answer D is the correct answer**. The facts of this question are taken from *Keiser v. Koester*, 1997 Neb. App. LEXIS 122 (Neb. Ct. App. 1997). As that court held, Arthur and Randall hold title to the lot as tenants in common. Evalyn then inherited Arthur's interest when he died. She then ousted Randall as a co-tenant due to her

adverse possession of the property for a period in excess of the statutory requirement. Evalyn had been in actual, continuous, exclusive, and notorious possession of the property under claim of ownership. By contrast, Randall had never occupied the property nor paid for taxes or improvements. He thus lost his interest in the land.

Answers A and B are incorrect because Evalyn's adverse possession would give her title regardless of the original status of that title. The conveyance "to Arthur and/or Randall" created a tenancy in common because that is the interested presumed in the absence of a contrary indication to create a joint tenancy. Arthur was allowed to devise his interest to Evalyn, so she and Randall owned the property as tenants in common until Evalyn ousted Randall by adverse possession. **Answer C is incorrect** because Randall lost title to the property via adverse possession.

106. **Answer D is the correct answer**. A statute of limitations presumes that it is inequitable to allow a cause of action to be brought after a certain period of time, so the potential plaintiff should act in a timely fashion rather than sleeping on its rights. The same rationale applies to landowners who neglect to protect their title by bringing a trespass action against an adverse possessor within the statutory period of time.

   Answer A is incorrect because the law does not judge real property more important than personal property, and even if it did, the rules for adverse possession are the same for land as they are for personal property. **Answer B is incorrect** because adverse possession is not designed to reward knowing trespassers. Indeed, some jurisdictions refuse to allow knowing trespassers from gaining title to land by adverse possession. **Answer C is incorrect** because the limitations of recording systems are relatively modest, and adverse possession applies whether or not title was clearly established pursuant to a recording statute.

107. **Answer A is the correct answer**. Julia's neighbor is responsible for the actions of her pet dog. The fact that no damage occurred to Julia's property does not matter, for a trespass action lies regardless of whether an actual injury is demonstrated.

   Answer B is incorrect because the courts are divided concerning the treatment of airborne particulates as a trespass. A minority of courts holds that objects of any size can commit a trespass, but the majority rule does not extend trespass actions to invisible particulates no matter how bothersome they are. A nuisance action will be available as an alternative. **Answer C is incorrect** because lights, like tiny particulates, are unlikely to be regarded as a trespass, although again there are some jurisdictions which may disagree. **Answer D is incorrect** because the exigent circumstances will justify the police's actions. Indeed, some courts have concluded that a police search that results in the seizure of property does not constitute a taking of the property seized, so the use of land to head off a fleeing bank robber is unlikely to give rise to a cause of action either.

108. **Answer B is the correct answer**. This problem is based upon *St. Paul Title Insurance Corp. v. Owen*, 452 So.2d 482 (Ala. 1984). Albert conveyed the land to Cheryl pursuant to a warranty deed, so Albert is liable for breach of the promise

contained in that deed. But the deed by which Cheryl conveyed the land to Dennis did not contain any such promise, so Cheryl is not liable based upon that deed.

Albert's liability explains why **Answers C and D are incorrect**; Cheryl's lack of liability explains why **Answers A and C are incorrect**.

109. **Answer D is the correct answer**. The remedy of forfeiture is only available when specifically authorized by statute, and no statute authorizes forfeiture as a remedy for trespass.

By contrast, **Answer A is incorrect** because imprisonment is a possibility for the felony of criminal trespass. **Answer B is incorrect** because monetary damages are a common remedy for a trespass. Likewise, **Answer C is incorrect** because ejectment is the other common remedy for a trespass.

110.   The best legal authority for Lisa's claim that she is entitled to keep her "Bush for President" sign is *Shelley v. Kraemer*, 334 U.S. 1 (1948), because it establishes that a covenant cannot be enforced if it violates the Constitution. *Shelley* held that the invocation of the judicial process to enforce the private covenant constituted state action subject to the equal protection clause. If *Shelley* is extended to the first amendment, then the restriction of election signs could be unconstitutional for the same reason. The courts have been reluctant to extend *Shelley*, though, so the success of Lisa's case is doubtful. Another good authority for Lisa is *City of LaDue v. Gilleo*, 512 U.S. 43 (1994), which holds that a municipal zoning ordinance can violate the first amendment if it restricts political signs. But *City of Ladue* addressed government zoning, not private covenants, so it is doubtful that Lisa will prevail on that theory either.

111.   The parking fee is probably invalid. *In Thanasoulis v. Winston Towers 200 Associates*, 542 A.2d 900 (N.J. 1988), the court considered a similar dispute. The court there acknowledged that a homeowner's association can establish reasonable parking regulations. But the court further held that an association cannot expropriate the economic value of an owner's parking space for its own use. An owner has the right to lease his or her unit, including the parking space and the interest in the common elements. Additionally, an association cannot discriminate against a nonresident owner assuming that the governing statute provides that an owner is only *proportionately liable* for his or her share of the common expenses. An association cannot require an owner to contribute three times more money to the common-expense fund for parking privileges than do other unit owners who do not rent their units.

112.   No, there is no easement that restricts Johansen's activities. An easement is a property interest that automatically runs with the land when it is conveyed to another party. An easement is extinguished by merger, however, if the holder of the easement obtains the fee simple interest in the land. Here BRCC first obtained the easement, and then it obtained the fee simple. But that fee simple was subject to a condition subsequent — the death of Campbell, who retained a life estate when she sold the land to BRCC. Accordingly, a merger did not occur when BRCC obtained the land. Upon Campbell's death, though, the life estate ended, and Johansen holds the land in fee simple. The requisite merger occurred because Johansen obtained all of the property interests held by BRCC, both the land and the easement.

113.   The courts which held that the presence of a cemetery in a residential neighborhood is not a nuisance questioned the nature of the harm asserted by the plaintiffs. The mere undesirability of the constant reminder of death evoked by a cemetery failed to impress some courts as the kind of injury that nuisance law addresses. Put differently, the fact that something is annoying does not mean that it is a nuisance.

Other courts explained that cemeteries must be located somewhere, so the community's interest outweighed any intangible complaints of the neighbors. It is true, though, that some courts accepted the argument that the constant reminder of death associated with a cemetery could support a nuisance claim, and that other complaints about cemeteries — most notably groundwater contamination — yielded more obvious nuisance actions. *See generally* John Copeland Nagle, *Moral Nuisances*, 50 Emory L.J. 265, 288-91 (2001) (citing cases).

114. Glen Theater's lawsuit against Growth Realty to recover the security deposit will likely fail. The agreement respecting the security deposit was between Glen Theater and Acme Realty. Therefore, Growth Realty is bound by that agreement only if it runs with the land. Glen Theater seeks to recover the money owed by the agreement, so it is seeking to enforce it as a real covenant. In most jurisdictions, one of the requirements for the enforcement of a real covenant (as well as an equitable servitude) is that the covenant must "touch and concern" the land. If a promise does not relate to land, there is no reason to require the next landowner to fulfill it. A security deposit will probably fail that test. Agreements for the payment of money are problematic under the touch and concern test, and the security deposit seems like it is more of personal agreement between Glen Theater and Growth Realty than it is related to the land.

115. **Answer D is the correct answer**. An easement by necessity is one of the four types of implied easements; otherwise an easement can only be created by the express agreement of the parties. Additionally, an easement by necessity can only arise upon the division of land that was previously owned by the same person. Even then, an easement by necessity exists only if it is necessary to use part of the divided land to gain access to the other parcel. Answer D describes such a situation.

Answer A is incorrect because use of land for any duration does not necessarily establish such a use is necessary. Nothing in Answer A indicates that the two neighboring parcels of land were once owned by the same party, either. **Answer B is incorrect** because convenience does not establish necessity, and again there is no evidence that the two neighboring parcels of land were once owned by the same party. **Answer C is incorrect** because it describes an express agreement negotiated by the parties, not an implied easement like an easement by necessity.

116. **Answer B is the correct answer**. One of the benefits of conveying a conservation easement is that the resulting restrictions on use should also reduce the value of the land for purposes of calculating property taxes. The conveyance of a conservation easement to a non-profit organization should also provide a charitable deduction.

Answer A is incorrect because a landowner can negotiate any price it chooses for a conservation easement. Even so, a landowner is highly unlikely to obtain the full market value of the property because the easement only conveys a limited right to the property. **Answer C is incorrect** because a landowner is still allowed to use the property subject to an easement, provided that the landowner does not interfere with the rights of the easement holder. The owner of land subject to a conservation easement will probably be allowed to engage in any activities that do not interfere with wildlife habitat, ecosystem health, scenic beauty, or other environmental values. Any other use of the property by the landowner will be permitted. **Answer D is incorrect** because a landowner is always allowed to sell property that is subject to an easement without the approval of the easement holder. The rule is no different for conservation easements.

117. **Answer A is the correct answer**. Peter wants his agreement with Elizabeth to run with the land. Moreover, he is seeking monetary damages, so he must satisfy the test for the enforcement of a real covenant. In some jurisdictions, horizontal privity is required for the burden of a real covenant to run with the land. Horizontal privity exists where the agreement occurs in conjunction with a transfer of an interest in any of the affected land. The fact that Peter and Elizabeth lived next to each other for five years does not represent the kind of relationship that horizontal privity requires.

    Answer B is incorrect because Peter and Elizabeth were in horizontal privity when they made the agreement. Nearly every state holds that horizontal privity exists if the covenant was agreed to at the time one party sold the property to the other. **Answers C and D are incorrect** because Peter is seeking an injunction, and thus the enforcement of an equitable servitude, but horizontal privity is not one of the requirements for an equitable servitude.

118. **Answer D is the correct answer** because Peggy has no right to use the land.

    Answer A is incorrect because a prescriptive easement requires similar criteria as adverse possession: the use of the land for the statutory period, exclusive use, open and notorious use, and use under a claim of right. Jim's use of Nancy's land was open, it appears to be exclusive, and it also appears to be under a claim of right. But he used the land for less than two years, which is far short of the statutory period established in any jurisdiction. **Answer B is incorrect** because no necessity to use the land arose at the time that the land was subdivided, and in any event, the use of land as a garden will not qualify as a necessity. **Answer C is incorrect** because there is no indication that Nancy ever misled Jim concerning his right to use the land, which is a prerequisite for the establishment of an easement by estoppel.

119. **Answer A is the correct answer**. There was no agreement between Lisa and Susan. Moreover, John did not own Greenacre at the time that he conveyed Yellowacre to Lisa. Accordingly, Lisa cannot rely upon an implied reciprocal easement because no such easement can attach to land after the original owner has conveyed it to someone else.

    Answer B is incorrect. In a jurisdiction that follows a third-party beneficiary theory, Susan could establish that she is a beneficiary of Lisa's promise not to use the land for a dog kennel. **Answer C is incorrect** because Susan could enforce the covenant as a successor to John. **Answer D is incorrect** because Jim's covenant benefited the land retained by John, and Lisa obtained the benefit of that covenant when she obtained Yellowacre.

120. **Answer C is the correct answer.** State right-to-farm statutes protect farmers from nuisance liability, and thus they afford a property right to farmers to engage in farming activities regardless of their effects. A neighbor who objects to the farm's activities will have to negotiate with the farm to surrender that property right rather than suing to hold the farm liable.

Answers A and B are incorrect because the farms protected by right-to-farm statutes are potential defendants, not plaintiffs. **Answer D is incorrect** because the statutes give farms a property right to engage in farming activities, not a right to hold those who interfere with such activities liable.

121. **Answer D is the correct answer.** A reciprocal negative easement exists when a sufficient number of lots in a subdivision contain the same covenant, so that the covenant will even be applied to the lots that are lacking them. A covenant limiting property to residential purposes is a common source of reciprocal negative easements, and such a covenant will block the use of Sandy's addition.

Answer A is incorrect because the mere fact that a previous owner used land for one purpose does not require a subsequent owner to use the land the same way. **Answer B is incorrect** because the mere assurance of a prior owner does not create a covenant that applies to other landowners, and that assurance does not give rise to a reciprocal negative easement either. **Answer C is incorrect** because the mere desires of a majority of landowners do not result in any actual restrictions.

122. **Answer C is the correct answer.** The wall separating Nancy's property from Andy is an example of a spite fence, which courts have declared a nuisance simply because of the hostile motive of the party building the fence. In other words, the utility of the conduct is near zero because its motive was improper.

Answer A is incorrect because the building of the fence does not constitute a nuisance per se. A nuisance per se exists only if an activity constitutes a nuisance in all times and places. **Answer B is incorrect** because the harm suffered by Billy and Andy is nearly the same, and a spite fence will be deemed a nuisance even if the harm is relatively modest. **Answer D is incorrect** because there is no indication whether Nancy or her neighbors moved there first, and again, Nancy would be liable for a spite fence even if she was there before Andy.

123. **Answer C is the correct answer.** Each of the answers presents questions concerning the satisfaction of the "touch and concern" requirement that most courts hold is necessary for a real covenant or an equitable servitude to run with the land. But the issue between Kim and Kara has nothing to do with whether their babysitting agreement runs with the land. Kara is seeking to enforce the agreement against Kim, the original party to the agreement. As such, the enforcement of the agreement presents a contract law question that does not depend at all upon the property interests of the parties, and while specific performance of that agreement might be unlikely, Kara might well be able to obtain a damages remedy.

Answer A is incorrect because a mortgage is a personal obligation to make a monetary payment which many jurisdictions will hold does not satisfy the touch and concern requirement for the agreement to run with the land. Likewise, whether or not an attorney's fee agreement satisfies the touch and concern test divides the courts, so **Answer B is incorrect. Answer D is incorrect** because it describes an affirmative obligation imposed upon Kim rather than a land use restriction. Affirmative covenants are more problematic under the touch and concern test because of several concerns about enforcing affirmative covenants against successors, including the reluctance of courts to issue orders that require continuing judicial supervision and the resemblance of affirmative obligations to anachronistic feudal service or perpetual rent.

124. **Answer A is the correct answer**. Horizontal privity is distinct from vertical privity. Horizontal privity refers to the relationship between the original parties to a covenant, while vertical privity describes the relationship between one of the original parties and its successors in ownership of the land. Thus horizontal privity is not duplicative of vertical privity.

    Answer B is incorrect because many jurisdictions have abandoned the horizontal privity requirement, and that could be a persuasive reason for additional jurisdictions to do so as well. **Answer C is incorrect** because the reasons for requiring horizontal privity are primarily historical, and the absence of any modern justification for those reasons provides another justification for abandoning horizontal privity. **Answer D is incorrect** because the existence of other tests for the enforceability of a covenant, especially simply focusing upon the intent of the original parties, offers yet another reason for a court to reject a horizontal privity requirement.

125. **Answer C is the correct answer**. If Eve had obtained an easement by necessity, that implied easement would have disappeared when the necessity disappeared. The new highway, in other words, would terminate the easement by necessity. But Eve did not obtain an implied easement by necessity; she obtained an express easement. That express easement will not end simply because Eve has an alternative route to reach her property.

    Answer A is incorrect because an easement holder's repeated abuse of the easement can result in the termination of the easement by forfeiture. **Answer B is incorrect** because Adam's intentional blockage of the road over twenty years ago will terminate the easement through prescription, which occurs if the servient owner uses the land adversely to the dominant owner for a sufficient period. **Answer D is incorrect** because of the merger doctrine, which posits that you cannot hold an easement across your own land.

126. **Answer D is the correct answer**. The express easement between Rob and Jerry extended to "ingress and egress to Jerry's property." The scope of that easement, therefore, does not encompass a right to vegetation, so **Answer A is incorrect**. Jerry cannot claim a prescriptive easement that entitles him to keep the trees, either, because there is no indication that Jerry planted and cared for the trees under a claim of right. Jerry may have thought he had a legal right to plant the trees, but he may have simply wanted to beautify the area provided that Rob did not object. The burden is on Jerry to establish a prescriptive easement, and the uncertainty will operate against him. Thus **Answers B and C are incorrect, too.**

127. **Answer B is the correct answer**. An easement by necessity arises only in circumstances when the dominant and servient tenement was once owned by the same person. Dawn's only options are to obtain an express easement or try to establish an easement by estoppel or an easement by prescription, but nothing in the facts suggests that she will satisfy the criteria for those two kinds of implied easements.

Answer A is incorrect because the failure to obtain an easement by the agreement of the landowner does not prejudice any claims that an implied easement has been established. **Answer C is incorrect** because it was not *necessary* to cross Jim's land when Patricia divided it; the fact that the traffic bothered Patricia will qualify as an annoyance, but not a necessity. **Answer D is incorrect** because the expense and difficulty that would attend Dawn's building such a road could persuade courts in some jurisdictions that it is practically impossible to leave Dawn's property in that manner, and therefore, crossing Jim's road is necessary.

128. **Answer B is the correct answer**. In many jurisdictions, including California, a covenant will be enforced by the courts provided that it is "reasonable." *See, e.g., Nahrstedt v. Lakeside Village Condominium Association, Inc.*, 878 P.2d 1275 (Cal. 1994). Concerns about the color of a couch inside someone's home could be deemed unreasonable because the interior color scheme bears little, and probably no, relationship to the interests of the community as a whole.

Answer A is incorrect because there is no equivalent of the zoning law of non-conforming uses that applies to covenants. **Answer C is incorrect** because there is no constitutional provision that directly addresses a right to choose how to decorate one's home, and more general liberty interests are unlikely to reach such questions as well. **Answer D is incorrect** because aesthetic concerns are often the basis for private covenants, and there is no legal rule that requires covenants and zoning to address separate issues.

129. **Answer C is the correct answer**. A reciprocal negative easement arises when most of the lots were burdened with the same covenant when the land was originally subdivided. The theory is that the presence of such covenants on most of the lots supports a finding that the covenants were intended to be reciprocal on all of the lots, including those that do not contain the express covenant in their deeds. Precisely how common the covenant must be to provide the notice and evidence of intent to establish a reciprocal negative easement is uncertain, but a restriction on 19 out of 21 lots is almost sure to qualify.

Answer A is incorrect because the term reciprocal negative "easement" is a misnomer: it refers to covenants, not to actual easements to use someone else's land. **Answer B is incorrect** because it addresses a conflict between two landowners, whereas a reciprocal negative easement requires evidence of the covenants applicable to an entire subdivision. **Answer D is incorrect** because it describes one of the few categories of negative easements, which is distinct from the concept of a reciprocal negative easement.

130. **Answer C is the correct answer**. The easement prohibited the landowner from acting contrary to the stated environmental concerns related to the old growth

forests. But the easement allowed the landowner to use the land in any other way that did not interfere with those forests. Eighteen Enterprises will thus be able to build its proposed golf course if it agrees not to use chemicals or otherwise interfere with the ecology and other environmental qualities of the land.

Answer A is incorrect because a landowner whose property is subject to an easement is still allowed to use that land in any way that does not interfere with the easement. **Answer B is incorrect** because the easement places an additional restriction upon Eighteen Enterprises's use of the land even if the government approves of the company's plans. Note, too, that any regulation of old growth forests occurring on privately owned land will likely be enacted by state or local governments because few federal regulations extend to such forests. **Answer D is incorrect** because easements run with the land, so Eighteen Enterprises must abide by the agreement between the Lewis family and NHF.

131.   **Answer D is the correct answer**. A covenant prohibiting flowers in the front yard of the burdened properties will likely be judged reasonable by the courts, especially given the deferential stance that most courts take toward private covenants.

By contrast, **Answer A is incorrect** because actual notice is not necessary for a covenant to run with the land; the inclusion of the covenant in the deed will suffice. **Answer B is incorrect** because a homeowner's association can regulate the use of properties, as demonstrated by the many judicial decisions upholding an association's enforcement of such a covenant. **Answer C is incorrect** because horizontal privity is never a requirement for an equitable servitude such as this one, where the homeowner's association seeks the equitable relief of an injunction.

132. Probably not. The city's traffic concerns are unlikely to constitute a compelling state interest under the new Religious Land Use and Institutionalized Persons Act (RLUIPA), 42 U.S.C. § 2000cc. According to RLUIPA, any governmental regulation of the land use of religious bodies must serve a compelling state interest and employ the least restrictive means of serving that interest. Even if the city's traffic concerns are judged to qualify as a compelling state interest, the church is likely to identify less restrictive means of regulating that traffic than an absolute ban on weddings and funerals. The constitutionality of RLUIPA has not been resolved yet, though, so the city will probably raise that issue in support of its zoning decision as well.

133. The federal Fair Housing Act offers Joe his best argument against the enforcement of the zoning ordinance. The FHA prohibits discrimination "against any person in the terms, conditions or privileges of rental or a dwelling because of a handicap of that renter." Discrimination is defined as "a refusal to make reasonable accommodations in rules, policies, practices, or services, when such accommodations may be necessary to afford such person equal opportunity to use and enjoy a dwelling." Joe's will assert that the city must allow him to build the fence in order to reasonably accommodate his post-traumatic stress disorder.

134. Carrie should apply for a variance from the regulations. In many jurisdictions, Carrie will need to establish both that she suffers an undue hardship from the existing zoning regulation and that a variance will not be detrimental to the area. If Carrie can make that showing, then she will be entitled to a variance. Alternatively, Carrie could seek to have the zoning changed, which is a common procedure but subject to charges of illegal spot zoning if the change affected only Carrie's lot. Or Carrie could simply redesign her planned house.

135. This problem is based upon *Blockbuster Videos, Inc. v. City of Tempe*, 141 F.3d 1295 (9th Cir. 1998). Tempe cannot enforce its ordinance because it conflicts with the federally protected trademark owned by Blockbuster. Generally, a community can employ zoning laws to regulate aesthetics, either by dictating the desired appearance or forbidding an unwanted appearance. But zoning law is state and local law, and it will always be subject to the command of the supremacy clause that federal laws trump contrary state laws. The federal Lanham Act protects trademarks like the one held by Blockbuster. Tempe's effort to modify the colors of Blockbuster's sign will thus fail because such zoning would interfere with the superior federally protected trademark held by Blockbuster.

136. The utilitarian theory of property best explains the changed perception of the federal public lands. During the nineteenth century, society placed the highest value on exploiting and extracting the natural resources contained on the public lands. By the end of the twentieth century, though, society also placed a great value on the

recreational and environmental values of those lands, while continuing to value the use of the mineral, timber, and other natural resources. The change in the law reflected a change in the perceived values of the land. In other words, society made a new utilitarian calculation respecting the best use of the public lands.

137. **Answer A is the correct answer.** Growth controls try to check rapid growth — or sometimes any growth — in a community out of concern for the effects such change can have on the existing lifestyle in that community. The premise is that the community's character will be preserved so long as the size of the community is unchanged, or at most has changed slowly.

      Answer B is incorrect because growth controls are not designed to keep housing prices down. In fact, they often have the opposite effect because property values will increase when fewer properties can be developed than the market would suggest. **Answer C is incorrect** because growth controls address a different issue than zoning laws. Growth controls limit any use of the land, while zoning merely specifies the kinds of uses that are permitted for the land. **Answer D is incorrect** because growth controls target all development in a particular area, whether or not the affected land uses would be viewed as nuisances. Thus growth controls restrict many land uses that would not be regarded as a nuisance.

138. **Answer C is the correct answer.** The notion of the public trust presupposes that the people once owned the property in their sovereign capacity. The public trust doctrine then operates to limit uses of the land that conflict with that trust, regardless of whether title to the land is now publicly or privately held.

      Answer A is incorrect because the eminent domain power authorizes the government to buy land or other property, whereas the public trust doctrine applies regardless of who owns the property. Indeed, the government may not need to exercise its eminent domain power if the restriction that it seeks to place upon property use is already contained in the public trust doctrine. Likewise, **Answer B is incorrect** because the public trust doctrine operates independently of the government's acquisition of land, no matter how the property is acquired. **Answer D is incorrect** because the police power provides distinct authority for the government to regulate land use. Land that is subject to a public trust already contains restrictions on land use, so the use of the police power may be unnecessary.

139. **Answer C is the correct answer** because both **Answers A and B are correct**. Spot zoning refers to a change in the zoning restrictions applicable to a specific parcel — or "spot" — of land like the 300 acres owned by Laura. Many jurisdictions view spot zoning unfavorably, though it will often be upheld if it satisfies a more rigorous judicial review of the zoning change. Conditional rezoning refers to the approval of a zoning change subject to certain conditions, like Laura's promise to contribute her private security forces to assist with conventions. Conditional rezoning is generally sustained — indeed, some state statutes expressly permit it — despite fears of undue influence and undermining the comprehensive plan. **Answer D is incorrect** because the decision to change the zoning can be described as both spot zoning and conditional rezoning (Answer (C)).

140. **Answer C is the correct answer.** Land that is used in a certain way at the time that a zoning law makes that use illegal is nonetheless protected as a nonconforming use. The rules for nonconforming uses seek to protect preexisting uses while controlling their expansion. **Answer C is correct** because the right to a nonconforming use runs with the land, so Pat will be able to operate the preschool there, too.

Answer A is incorrect because a store is a different use than a school, and the nonconforming status will not continue if the land is used for a different purpose. **Answer B is incorrect** because an addition is likely to be viewed as an expansion of the use that exceeds the original nonconforming use. **Answer D is incorrect** because the action described in Answer (C) will most likely be permitted.

141. **Answer B is the correct answer**. A special exception is a use permitted by the ordinance in a district where it is not necessarily incompatible, but where it might cause harm if not watched. The idea, as expressed in Answer B, is that certain uses are desirable and appropriate for a zone, but not at every location or without conditions being attached. Common examples of special exceptions include a hospital in a residential district and a gas station in a light commercial district.

Answer A is incorrect because the notion of special exceptions is not that the zoning board should always retain a generalized power to decide whether or not to allow a proposed use on a case-by-case basis. **Answer C is incorrect** because special exceptions do not grant the zoning board the power to consider any proposed use of land, but rather only those few uses that have been predetermined to be acceptable in a designated zone provided that the fit with the precise location is satisfactory. **Answer D is incorrect** because special exceptions are exceptions to the zoning ordinance, not the comprehensive plan.

142. **Answer B is the correct answer**. A nonconforming use may be transferred to another owner so long as the use remains the same.

Answer A is incorrect because the six years that have lapsed since Al's All-Nighter last operated will be deemed to be an abandonment of the nonconforming use, which cannot be revived once it is abandoned. The 2000 zoning ordinance will now govern any use of the land. **Answer C is incorrect** because it describes a significant addition that is beyond the scope of the nonconforming use. **Answer D is incorrect** because the right to a nonconforming use is limited to the particular use that existed at the time the zoning law was enacted. The sale of donuts is a different use from the sale of hardware products, so the latter will not be included within the right to the nonconforming use.

143. **Answer D is the correct answer** because **Answers A, B, and C are all incorrect**.

Answer A is incorrect because there is no uniform treatment of the effect of conflicts of interest on the resulting zoning decisions. While many jurisdictions will invalidate a zoning amendment that was adopted by a council with a member who owned some of the affected land, not every jurisdiction will remedy that conflict by striking the zoning provision itself. **Answer B is incorrect** because few jurisdictions afford much teeth to the concept of the comprehensive plan, and the reality that zoning amendments frequently yield changes that are inconsistent with the plans has not caused the courts to invalidate such amendments. **Answer C is incorrect** because few states have followed the lead of Oregon in *Fasano v. Board of County Commissioners of Washington County*, 507 P.2d 23 (Or. 1973), which treated zoning amendments as adjudicative actions susceptible to a more stringent standard of judicial review than legislative actions.

144.   **Answer D is the correct answer**. Generally, a variance is available to a landowner who establishes that it will suffer an undue hardship from the ordinary application of the zoning law and that a variance will not be detrimental to the area in which the land is located. That Chuck wants to build a house that is similar to the others in the neighborhood suggests that a variance will not be detrimental to that area. The fact that Chuck only wants to build a one-bedroom house indicates that he might not be able to build anything on the land if the zoning law is strictly enforced, so that he would suffer an undue burden if he is not able to do so. Chuck could also be helped in his case by the fact that he has owned the small lot since before the zoning law, which could suggest that the zoning does not really fit the small lot that Chuck owns. Finally, variances tend to be easier to get for the set back and minimum lot provisions that Chuck confronts, and more difficult for use restrictions.

   Answer A is incorrect because McDonald's purchased the lot 43 years after the area was zoned with knowledge that only residential uses were permitted. That knowledge will make it much more difficult for McDonald's to get a variance. **Answer B is incorrect** because the undue burden that Frank could suffer is not matched by any evidence that the apartments will fit into the neighborhood. Frank is allowed to build a single-family residence, so his inability to recover his investment might be due to paying too much for the land. **Answer C is incorrect** because there is no evidence that Al will suffer an undue burden if he cannot build a store but must continue to have a house there instead.

145.   **Answer C is the correct answer**. The Supreme Court has upheld two different kinds of zoning ordinances addressing adult book stores and theaters: an ordinance like that in Answer A which requires the dispersal of such facilities throughout the area, and an ordinance like Answer B that requires the concentration of such facilities in a particular area. The two ordinances reflect diametrically different conclusions concerning the best manner to reduce the negative effects associated with adult book stores and theaters, but the Court has held that the choice between those approaches is within the discretion of the local community. Therefore, both **Answers A and B are incorrect**, so **Answer C is the correct answer**, and **Answer D is incorrect**.

146.   **Answer A is the correct answer**. The building is likely to be judged a nonconforming use because it had been there long before the town enacted a zoning law in 1950. Moreover, the particular zoning regulation at issue here addresses the distance between a building and the road. The building in question qualifies as a nonconforming use with respect to that requirement. The use of the building as a home instead of a barn in no way affects the status of the building under the setback requirement. The result might be different if the relevant zoning regulation was a

restriction on the use of the property, instead of its location, but the fact that it is only a setback restriction shifts the focus to whether the building is moved — it is not — instead of how the building is to be used.

Answer B is incorrect because there is no evidence that the Miserocchi's will suffer an undue hardship if they are unable to convert the barn into a home. **Answer C is incorrect** because there is no indication that the land is subject to a special exception under the town's zoning law. **Answer D is incorrect** because a takings claim will likely fail since the property will still be valuable, even though it might be less valuable with a barn than with a home.

147.   **Answer B is the correct answer**. There is little precedent for treating the destruction of wildlife habitat as a private nuisance. The fact that wild animals are not owned until they are captured further complicates any effort to protect such habitat by nuisance law. Some commentators have argued that private nuisance law should reach such cases, but so far the courts have not done so.

Answer A is incorrect because the government's purchase of wildlife habitat is a common method of protecting endangered species. Many such purchases are voluntary, but eminent domain will be available because the protection of endangered species qualifies as a public use for purposes of the fifth amendment's takings clause. **Answer C is incorrect** because easements, and particularly conservation easements, are another common means of protecting wildlife habitat. **Answer D is incorrect** because zoning law can be used to restrict development that would interfere with wildlife habitat or other environmental values, such as wetlands.

148.   **Answer D is the correct answer**.

Answer A is incorrect because a ban on billboards might survive first amendment scrutiny. Commercial speech receives less protection than other speech, so a ban on billboards could be constitutional if the government articulates a sufficient purpose and the effect of such a ban is minimized. **Answer B is incorrect** because the Supreme Court has upheld restrictions on the number of unrelated people who live in a house. See *Village of Belle Terre v. Boraas*, 416 U.S. 1 (1974). **Answer C is incorrect** because a restriction on the size of buildings is within the zoning power. Moreover, zoning laws may be enacted by popular initiatives, though they may receive heightened judicial scrutiny. The fact that Answers (A), (B), and (C) are incorrect makes Answer (D) the correct answer.

149.   **Answer A is the correct answer**. Aesthetic regulations are within the scope of the zoning power. A particular scheme for regulating aesthetics is most likely to survive if it provides sufficient guidance to those responsible for enforcing it. The reference to Art Deco design features provides an objective standard that the city's architectural board can apply without being arbitrary. Therefore, that standard will doom Jenny's challenge to the board's refusal to approve her plans.

Answer B is incorrect because a zoning board need not retain a nationally recognized expert in order to apply an aesthetic zoning standard. It is the precision of the standard itself that is most important, not the national qualifications of the people charged with enforcing it. **Answer C is incorrect** because very few courts have held that the application of an aesthetic zoning standard violates a constitutional right to freedom of expression. Some commentators have supported greater constitutional protection for aesthetic choices, but the courts have been reluctant to extend such protection so far. **Answer D is incorrect** because today nearly every jurisdiction holds that the police power includes the power to regulate aesthetics. That was not the case early in the twentieth century when a number of courts invalidated zoning provisions and other government regulations aimed at controlling aesthetics. But such decisions are rare today, and aesthetic regulations are common.

150. **Answer D is the correct answer.** According to section 821B of the Restatement (Second) of Torts, a public nuisance is "an unreasonable interference with a right common to the general public." "Unreasonable," in turn, can mean either a "significant interference with public health, safety, comfort or convenience" or an activity that is "illegal." *Id.* Hazardous substances often become public nuisances as they enter the groundwater, migrate onto neighboring land, or even threaten to harm the public. But if the drums on LRC's land are neither leaking nor corroded, then they do not pose an immediate threat to the surrounding community, and they will not be a public nuisance.

Answer A is incorrect because the owner of property is responsible for a public nuisance regardless of the owner's knowledge or involvement in the creation of that nuisance. Public nuisance liability attaches on the basis of land ownership, not for causation of the offending condition. **Answer B is incorrect** because a public nuisance exists even with the threat of harm to the community; the state does not have to wait for the neighbors to be injured before it can seek to abate the nuisance. The leaking barrels suggest that the community is threatened. **Answer C is incorrect** because the law of public nuisances operates independently of environmental law, so a particular activity might violate one or the other, or neither, or both.

151. **Answer D is the correct answer.** Conditional rezoning occurs when the zoning board changes the zoning law at a party's request, but adds conditions to that change that the party must satisfy in order to proceed with its planned activity. Conditional rezoning minimizes the potentially harmful effect of a zoning change on the neighborhood in a way that provides the maximum flexibility to the zoning authorities.

Answer A is incorrect because conditional zoning sometimes authorizes activities that are not in strict compliance with the comprehensive plan. **Answer B is incorrect** because the municipal zoning authorities decide whether or not to engage in conditional rezoning, not the courts. **Answer C is incorrect** because it describes contract zoning as opposed to conditional rezoning. Contract rezoning involves an enforceable reciprocal agreement with the local government, while conditional rezoning does not involve any commitments by the local government.

152. **Answer A is the correct answer.** A floating zone occurs when zoning law authorizes a use in the abstract but waits for a specific proposal to determine where

that use may occur. Such a zone affords a city flexibility by authorizing the use before committing to the precise location for that use.

Answer B is incorrect because a floating zone does not require the zoning board to change its mind. Rather, the initial approval of the zone is simply subject to subsequent clarification about where it will be located. Moreover, it is the municipal legislative body that creates a floating zone, not the administrative zoning board. **Answer C is incorrect** because it describes conditional rezoning instead of a floating zone. **Answer D is incorrect** because a floating zone is unrelated to the size of the jurisdiction subject to zoning, and such a zone does not presuppose any changes in that size.

153. **Answer C is the correct answer.** The statutes governing national forests direct the United States Forest Service to encourage the "multiple use" of those forests. Logging, recreation, grazing, wilderness, mining, wildlife habitat, and numerous other uses are to be approved by the Forest Service, albeit not all at the same place and the same time.

Answer A is incorrect because the Forest Service's authority is constrained by the statutes enacted by Congress, and those statutes do not afford the Forest Service to simply exclude any uses that it does not like. **Answer B is incorrect** because Congress has provided specific directions to the Forest Service concerning the management of national forests, so any agency decisions contrary to those direction are subject to reversal in court. **Answer D is incorrect** because Congress has given the federal courts subject matter jurisdiction to resolve most disputes about the management of public lands. Who may bring such lawsuits — *i.e.*, who has standing — remains controversial in some instances, but the general authority of the courts to review the Forest Service's decisions exists in most cases.

154. This is the question that was presented in *El-Shifa Pharmaceuticals Industries Co. v. United States*, 55 Fed. Cl. 751 (2003). The court held that "[t]he constitutional protection afforded by the Takings Clause is not intended to compensate for destruction of enemy war-making property through the exercise of military force." If that were not the rule, then presumably the United States would have been liable for massive numbers of takings of German and Japanese property during World War II, and most recently for takings of Iraqi property in 2003. The best analogy is to the cases holding that the government does not commit a taking when it destroys some houses to stop the progress of an oncoming fire that could destroy an entire city. Alternately, it is still an open question whether the takings clause ever applies to American actions in other countries, but the Court of Federal Claims assumed that it could at least in some circumstances. But not for purposeful military actions during a war.

155. The city probably has to compensate Mekuria. The facts of this question are taken from *Mekuria v. Washington Metropolitan Area Transit Authority*, 45 F. Supp. 2d 19 (D.D.C. 1999). The court there held that the construction of the Metro inflicted serious economic harm by interfering with Mekuria's business to such a degree that he was forced to either close the business or incur substantial losses. As such, there was no total taking of Mekuria's property, but Mekuria prevailed under the general takings balancing test. In particular, the court held that the city interfered with the plaintiff's distinct investment-backed expectations. While Mekuria could not be sure that his business would succeed, he could expect that he and his patrons would have reasonable access to his business. But the court noted that any businesses that renewed their leases during the course of the construction of the Metro did not suffer a diminution of their expectations during that time following the lease renewals.

156. Takings jurisprudence examines the effect of the government's actions on a property owner's rights. In several instances, whether a regulation constitutes a taking depends upon which property rights are affected by the regulation. For example, if a regulation takes all of an owner's property, then a per se rule states that a taking has occurred. But if the owner still retains valuable rights to use the property — perhaps for a home instead of large commercial building, or even transferable development rights that can be used elsewhere — the continued existence of some rights could defeat the takings claim. Takings law also gives priority to one of the rights in the bundle — the right to exclude — by holding that any physical invasion of private property by the government also constitutes a taking. Takings law's treatment of nuisances further illustrates the bundle of sticks analogy. A taking does not occur if a government regulation simply responds to a common law nuisance because the ability to engage in a nuisance was never one of the rights in a property owner's bundle.

157.   The county can claim that the government does not "take" land for purposes of the takings clause when it obtains title to the land by adverse possession. Ordinarily, the government gains title to property either by negotiating with the owner or by condemning it through the eminent domain power, and in such cases the payment requirement ensures that the government will not simply take what it should have paid for. But adverse possession is a different way of obtaining title to property. Adverse possession invokes the statute of limitations against the original owner for failure to adequately protect its rights. Most importantly, compensation is not required when private parties gain title to land by adverse possession, so the county can argue that the government should not have to pay either. All of that said, the courts are divided on whether the government must pay just compensation for land that it acquires through adverse possession.

158.   The state courts which have held that the seizure of private property by the police executing a search warrant does not constitute a taking advanced several arguments. They rely upon the government's police power to protect the safety of the community. They cite the longstanding English rule that the public has the right to everyone's evidence; stated differently, the duty to provide evidence is inherent in citizenship. They balance the respective interests by emphasizing the ubiquity of searches and the necessity of seizing evidence would render any takings claims incredibly burdensome to the government. They note that a rule requiring compensation would also find a taking whenever the government interferes with someone's liberty by directing them to testify in court. They insist that the legislature is better situated to apportion the burdens and benefits of public life than judicial adjudication of the takings clause.

159.   **Answer C is the correct answer**. A requirement that a homeowner plant a garden on his or her land constitutes a physical invasion of that property by the government. In *Loretto v. Teleprompter Manhattan CATV Corp.*, 458 U.S. 419 (1982), the Supreme Court held that a government mandate that an apartment owner allow a cable television box on the side of his building constituted a taking. Santa Rosa's garden requirement would be a taking for the same reason.

        Answer A is incorrect because the release of chemicals by the dry cleaning shop constitutes a nuisance. A property owner does not have a right to engage in a nuisance, so the government can abate that nuisance without taking anything from the landowner. **Answer B is incorrect** because it is possible — though not certain — that the exaction imposed by the city will satisfy the nexus and proportionality tests developed by the Supreme Court. **Answer D is incorrect** because a tax is not a taking.

160.   **Answer B is the correct answer**. The extent of the police power determines the extent of what qualifies as a public use. If the government is empowered to act, then it can use its eminent domain power for that action.

        Answer A is incorrect because the prevailing test for what constitutes a "public use" considers why the government wants to take the property. If that purpose is in the public interest, then the public use test is satisfied. That test thus focuses on the government's ends, not the government's means. The minority rule considers whether the government itself will actually use the property, as opposed to the government's acquiring the property for use by others. **Answer C is incorrect** because a taking need not involve the government actually acquiring the property. A regulatory taking in which a land use restriction is deemed to constitute a taking of the affected land nonetheless satisfies the public use test. **Answer D is incorrect** because the Supreme Court's unanimous decision in *Hawaii Housing Authority v. Midkiff*, 467 U.S. 229 (1984), endorsed the broader view of a public use.

161. **Answer B is the correct answer**. The scriptural teaching refers to how land should be used, so the government — like all owners — should use land in a manner that benefits others. If the government is not a good steward, the argument continues, then the government should not own that land.

     Answer A is incorrect because the eminent domain power does not presuppose that all land belonged to the government at one time. Rather, the eminent domain power presumes that the government should have the power to acquire land that it needs, whether or not it had owned that land before. **Answer C is incorrect** because the scriptural teaching does not address the theoretical issue concerning the government's duty to pay for land that it condemns. **Answer D is incorrect** because the stewardship duty does not establish such a heightened test for the government acquiring land; the suggestion instead is that the government can acquire land that it can use in a wise fashion.

162. **Answer C is the correct answer**. The fact that Donna can still use her property, even for a 50-story building, demonstrates that she has not suffered a total taking of her property that qualifies as a taking in every instance. Donna will also lose according to the balancing test that governs regulatory takings generally because of the government's interest in regulating the height of buildings, because the regulation is preexisting, and because a building of that size is unprecedented by her own admission.

     Answer A is incorrect because the ad coelum doctrine is not applied so strictly as to deem any government regulation of the height of buildings or other structures a taking. Typically, ad coelum is viewed more flexibly, and it is only infrequently determinative in takings cases. **Answer B is incorrect** because zoning has long been concerned with the height of buildings, and such regulations have long been sustained. **Answer D is incorrect** because there is nothing to suggest that the height of the building renders it a nuisance. A private nuisance would exist only if another landowner could show that it suffered a substantial interference with the use and enjoyment of its land.

163. **Answer C is the correct answer**. The commercial and military flights would constitute a nuisance if they are so low and so harmful that they substantially interfere with Ralph's use and enjoyment of his land. The military flights could constitute a taking in two different ways. First, the impact upon Ralph's use of his land might be so great that his property is rendered worthless, so a total taking of Ralph's property occurs. Second, the flights could be seen as effectively taking

an easement above Ralph's property, which is the theory that the Supreme Court relied upon in the analogous case of *United States v. Causby*, 328 U.S. 256 (1946). Of course, the flights might not be so bothersome to qualify as either a nuisance or a taking; further development of the facts would be necessary to decide that. But the fact that both a takings claim and a nuisance claim might be available to Ralph means that **Answer C is the correct answer**, while **Answers A, B, and D are all incorrect**.

164.   **Answer A is the correct answer**. Intellectual property, including copyrights and trademarks, are subject to the takings clause, so the government must compensate intellectual property owners when it takes their property. Copyright law and trademark law both give the property owner the right to license any — or no — uses of the property. Here the government used the AFA's web site, which could be protected by both copyright and trademark law. Government use of property constitutes a taking without need to consider any balancing tests or the more generalized equities of the dispute.

   Answer B is incorrect because an important public purpose does not eliminate the requirement that the government pay for the property that it takes. The congressional purpose will provide evidence that the public use test is satisfied, but just compensation is still due. **Answer C is incorrect** because web site designs are property — they may be copyrighted, they may employ protected trademarks, and they may even contain patented features (though there is no evidence of that in this case). **Answer D is incorrect** because government use of property constitutes a taking, even if the property owner has suffered a very minor loss. In *Loretto v. Teleprompter Manhattan CATV Corp.*, 458 U.S. 419 (1982), for example, the Supreme Court held that a taking occurred when the city used an apartment building for the location of a cable television box, even though the resulting compensation was determined to be just one dollar.

165.   **Answer B is the correct answer**. The typical measure of just compensation is the fair market value of the property. One of the best ways to determine fair market value is to rely upon the expertise of local real estate agents who are familiar with the private market for similar properties. Of course, different real estate agents may appraise the value of the property differently, but the sole appraisal contained in the answers to this question will be the best evidence of the fair market value of the AWA's property.

   Answer A is incorrect because replacement costs are not included within a just compensation award. Replacement cost is not part of the fair market value, which is the lodestar for determining just compensation. A few cases have awarded replacement costs in takings cases, but such awards are very unusual. **Answer C is incorrect** because the fact that the government could have built a less expensive park somewhere else does not mean that the government can limit its costs for the land that it does choose. Again, fair market value is based upon the private market for the land in question, not the cost of a specialized use in unrelated places. **Answer D is incorrect** because the fifth amendment and state constitutional provisions each require that the government pay just compensation whenever it acquires property, and the property here is certainly not worthless.

166. **Answer D is the correct answer**. The county's regulation reduces the value of Aaron's and Brandon's land, but it does not make it worthless. Accordingly, their regulatory takings claim will be judged by the balancing test articulated in *Penn Central Transportation Co. v. City of New York*, 438 U.S. 104 (1978). The government's interests in historic preservation and public safety, along with the continued value of Aaron's and Brandon's land given that they can still access it by an admittedly more circuitous route, will operate to defeat a takings claim.

    Answer A is incorrect because the prohibition on using the bridge furthers the county's dual interests in historic preservation and in public safety. These exercises of the police power demonstrate that the restriction upon the use of the land qualifies as a public use, too, under the prevailing understanding of the public use requirement. **Answer B is incorrect** because the *Armstrong* principle's general teaching that the government pays when fairness dictates does not operate as a general rule for adjudicating takings disputes. *See Armstrong v. United States*, 364 U.S. 40, 49 (1960). **Answer C is incorrect** because a regulatory taking occurs when government regulations have a sufficiently adverse effect upon a property owner. The government must pay just compensation for a regulatory taking regardless of the beneficial purpose of the regulation.

167. **Answer C is the correct answer**. The navigation servitude functions as a property right to continued navigation of the waterways that empowers the government to vindicate that right by clearing a waterway. The characterization as a servitude implies its nature as a property right held by the government. The source of that right is unclear — indeed, it might be an exercise of the police power — but those who own land or minerals beneath navigable waterways should be aware of the government's longstanding interest.

    Answer A is incorrect because interferences with navigation do not necessarily constitute a nuisance. They might; but they might not, too. **Answer B is incorrect** because private ownership of the land and minerals beneath navigable waterways is permitted. **Answer D is incorrect** because the fact that the government pays to keep waterways clear does not insulate the government from takings liability. For example, if the government comes onto your land to clear a path through the woods, the benefit resulting from that path will not preclude a takings claim based upon the government's physical invasion of your land.

168. **Answer A is the correct answer**. In regulatory takings law, the denominator problem refers to the difficulty in identifying the specific property that is affected by the city's regulation. Alicia will argue that the city has taken all three of its remaining acres, or 100% of her remaining land, which qualifies as a total taking for which compensation is due. The city, by contrast, will insist that the regulation has affected only three of Alicia's twenty acres, or 15% of her land, which falls far short of a total taking and is thus subject to the more flexible balancing test. In each instance, the numerator is the same — three — but the opposing denominators of three and twenty account for the radically different calculations of the fraction of the land that the city's regulation affects.

    Answer B is incorrect because there is no dispute about the amount of land affected by the state's wetlands regulation — all fifty acres are affected. Whether or not the wetlands work a taking is uncertain, but that question is distinct from the denominator problem. **Answer C is incorrect** because the city's exercise of its eminent domain power may raise questions concerning the motivation of the city in taking land from a religious organization, but that does not implicate the denominator problem. **Answer D is incorrect** because it describes an exaction, which raises a distinct takings issue from the denominator problem as well. The courts will analyze the constitutionality of the city's exaction by considering the nexus and proportionality to the city's interests, rather than engaging in the judgment about the fraction of the property affected in order to resolve the denominator problem.

169.   **Answer C is the correct answer**. Conditioning approval of the project upon an agreement to build on certain lands will constitute an exaction subject to constitutional scrutiny under the takings clause. But this exaction should satisfy both the nexus test — for the relationship between flooding and not building is easy to establish — and the proportionality test — because setting aside one quarter of the company's land seems sufficiently related to the flooding concerns. Moreover, the exaction here differs from the one at issue in *Dolan v. City of Tigard*, 512 U.S. 374 (1994), because the city in *Dolan* sought to actually obtain title to the property rather than simply restricting building there.

   Answer A is incorrect because in an eminent domain proceeding the city would have to pay the higher price of the fair market value of the land for the kinds of businesses that have traditionally operated there; the city could not pay the lesser value of the land as a park, nor could it rezone the land in an indirect effort to reduce its value for eminent domain purposes. **Answer B is incorrect** because the requirement that the company allow shops to be built upon its land will probably fail both parts of the test for exactions stated in *Dolan*. **Answer D is incorrect** because interference with economic development does not constitute a public nuisance.

170.   **Answer A is the correct answer** because the wells would constitute a physical invasion of Julia's land, for which compensation is automatically required.

   By contrast, **Answer B is incorrect** because the enforcement of the state historical preservation statute is unlikely to qualify as a regulatory taking. Julia's home will retain significant value, so the regulation does not work a total taking of her property. Moreover, the state's interests, Julia's expectations, and the extent of the regulation suggest that there will not be a taking according to the balancing test stated in *Penn Central Transportation Co. v. City of New York*, 438 U.S. 104 (1978). **Answer C is incorrect** because it, too, will likely fail to be deemed a regulatory taking under *Penn Central*. Julia's plan itself does not demonstrate the investment-backed expectations that could suggest that a taking has occurred. **Answer D is incorrect** because governmental destruction of property that threatens the public safety and health has long been deemed to be permissible without triggering the duty to compensate the affected property owner.

171. The Lakefront Industrial Corporation owns the land in fee simple. Charlotte attempted to convey a fee simple determinable to Lakefront with a shifting executory interest to Washington County. But Washington County's interest violates the Rule against Perpetuities. It is possible that Lakefront could allow the public to hike on the property for 200 years -in other words, more than 21 years after the life of anyone alive at the time of the conveyance -and then deny such public access. The executory interest thus may not vest or fail within 21 years after the life of anyone in being at the time of the conveyance. Moreover, although some jurisdictions do not apply the Rule against Perpetuities if both parties are charities, Lakefront is not a charity.

172. Patriot will probably succeed. 42 U.S.C. § 1983 provides a federal cause of action to those who are deprived of their property without due process of law. The threshold question is whether Patriot held a constitutionally protected property interest. In most jurisdictions, courts have held that a landowner has a protected property interest in a prior zoning classification, especially if the landowner has acted in reliance upon that classification. The next question is whether the county deprived Patriot of that interest without providing the requisite process. The revocation of a permit without any opportunity to appeal probably does not afford the due process required by the fourteenth amendment. The county could argue that Patriot should have opposed the zoning change, but Patriot could respond that it did not know that the change would result in the immediate revocation of its permit without affording Patriot an opportunity to qualify as a nonconforming use, to seek a variance, or to find some alternative grounds for relief.

173. It does not appear that any court has had the occasion to apply other fundamental theories of property law to weather modification activities, but it is possible to imagine how those theories would apply. An occupation theory posits that property ownership occurs when something is captured and reduced to possession, so occupation theory would suggest that precipitation is not owned until someone captures it. Occupation theory might actually affirm the legitimacy of weather modification programs that "capture" precipitation before it reaches the earth. Likewise, labor theory could approve such programs because labor theory would honor the mix of a natural resource and the effort undertaken to improve it. Utilitarian theory would consider the reasonable expectations of the affected parties, which could support the claims of those seeking a natural level of precipitation, but which could also provoke a heated disagreement about the ability to modify the weather. It is more difficult to conceive how economic theories of property might apply to weather modification programs, in part because of the variety of such theories, but general wealth maximization principles could support the use of weather modification programs if they help some landowners more than they harm others.

174. Hilda will be able to keep the ring, but not the piano or the home. She will be able to keep the ring because Sylvester intended to give it to her, delivered it to her,

and did not voice any conditions upon her keeping it. She will probably not be able to keep the piano because Sylvester did not deliver it to her. She could argue that the delivery of such a large item located so far away did not require an actual delivery, but Sylvester's failure to provide any other tangible evidence of his intentions -such as a letter explaining the gift -makes it unlikely that the delivery requirement was satisfied. It is even questionable whether Sylvester demonstrated the requisite intent to make the gift because he told Hilda that she still needed to "choose which piano she wanted." Hilda will not be able to keep the home because it was a failed gift causa mortis. Sylvester gave Hilda the deed to his mountain home because he thought he was about to die. In fact, he lived. So while three of the requirements of a gift causa mortis were satisfied -intent, apprehension of death, and delivery -the fourth criteria -actual death -was not satisfied.

175. The policies supporting the right of publicity probably do not support the claims of President Jackson's descendants. Courts have identified a number of policies supporting the extension of the right of publicity to the descendants of a famous person. Some of those policies support the claims of President Jackson's descendants. Other kinds of property are descendible, and third parties should not be able to reap what someone else has sown. But most of the policies are absent in the case of the Andrew Jackson car wash. There is no evidence that President Jackson worked to direct the future exploitation of his fame, or that he intentionally cultivated a persona in order to benefit his heirs. There are no existing contracts involving Jackson that would be affected by the failure to recognize his right of publicity more than 150 years after his death, nor is the public likely to be confused into believing that Jackson (or his descendants) have carefully decided which commercial opportunities to exploit and which to decline. Any concerns about unfair competition are absent in this instance, too.

176. Big Casinos Developer will probably have to pay the impact fee. The validity of the fee will probably be judged by the constitutional test for exactions stated by the Supreme Court in *Dolan v. City of Tigard*, 512 U.S. 374 (1994). According to that test, there must be an essential nexus between legitimate state interests and the conditions imposed upon the development, and there must be a rough proportionality between the conditions and the projected impact of the proposed development. The nexus test would appear to be satisfied here because the use of the funds for public roads, sewer lines, water supplies, public art, and other county infrastructure are related to the county's concerns about traffic, pollution, crime, and cost of housing. The rough proportionality test is likely satisfied, too, because an impact fee of $2,750 per residence seems like a reasonable amount to charge for the services that the development will require. Note, too, that it is not entirely clear whether monetary fees are subject to the constitutional test for exactions, so the fee will be even more likely to survive if that test is not applicable.

177. Big Casino Developers will probably succeed in its plan to build the homes for the compulsive gamblers, but it is difficult to be too confident in that result. At the outset, it is not certain that Section 2 of the CCGCA applies to the homes because that provision does not specifically mention compulsive gamblers. It is likely, though, that the reference to those "recovering from substance abuse or another disorder"

would encompass compulsory gamblers. The CCGCA would thus limit the group homes to eight residents, not the 25 sought by the developer. But the federal Fair Housing Act relates to this issue because that statute prohibits housing discrimination against the disabled. Compulsive gamblers probably qualify as disabled, although again that conclusion is not certain. Assuming that the FHA does apply, the county will stress that the FHA exempts "any reasonable local, State or Federal restrictions regarding the maximum number of occupants permitted to occupy a dwelling." In *City of Edmonds v. Oxford House, Inc.*, 514 U.S. 725 (1995), the Supreme Court held that the FHA distinguishes between permissible maximum occupancy rules and impermissible rules defining the family character of permissible land uses in a neighborhood. Section 2 of the CCGCA could be read as either governing maximum occupancy or as regulating the character of the community, and the general purposes of the CCGCA cut both ways as well, with stated concerns about population growth and about quality of life. Given the closeness of the question, the Court's admonition that exemptions from the FHA should be read narrowly because of the broad policy goals of the statute could resolve the case in favor of the invalidity of Section 2 of the CCGCA as applied to the proposed homes for compulsive gamblers.

178. Beth will probably not be able to build the development of vacation homes on the 20,000 acres of land. The conveyance created a tenancy in common between Celia, Suzanne, and Beth because today most states presume such a tenancy results from a conveyance to concurrent owners that does not specify otherwise. In other words, a tenancy in common is presumed instead of a joint tenancy. Each cotenant is entitled to use the entire premises provided that they do not interfere with the rights of their cotenants. Thus Beth will be able to build a development only if it does not interfere with the rights of Celia and Suzanne. Beth might be able to build a house without interfering with their rights, but a development containing luxury vacation homes is much more likely to interfere with Celia's and Suzanne's right to use the land as they wish by keeping it pristine. If the cotenants fail to agree, then Beth can pursue a partition action which will end the tenancy in common and give each party an equal share of the 20,000 acres. Beth, therefore, could probably build her desired development, but not until the 20,000 acres are partitioned.

179. Joyce owns the possessory right to both lots. Dickson's conveyance of the first lot attempted to give Andrea another fee simple subject to a condition subsequent with Boris receiving a shifting executory interest. That interest is void, though, because it could vest or fail at any time in the future that liquor is sold on the premises, including a time past 21 years after any life in being at the time of the conveyance. Accordingly, Andrea received a fee simple absolute that continues even though she sells coffee on the land. Dickson's conveyance of the second lot resulted in Andrea receiving a fee simple subject to a condition subsequent with Dickson retaining a right of reentry. The "but if" language made the conveyance subject to a condition subsequent rather than a fee simple determinable. The right of reentry is held by the grantor and is thus exempt from the Rule against Perpetuities. But Andrea has not sold liquor on the premises (assuming that none of the coffee drinks contain alcohol), so she continues to own the possessory right to that lot as well.

180. Yes, the covenant prohibits Global from operating a convenience store. The covenant satisfies the standard criteria for the enforcement of an equitable servitude: the parties intended for it to apply to Speedy's successors; there is vertical privity between Speedy and Global Food, and between Mom's Family Restaurant and Food Now; and the agreement about the commercial activity on the property touches and concerns the land. Global will want to argue that changed conditions preclude the enforcement of the agreement. Specifically, Global can point to the common practice of gas stations combining with convenience stores, unlike the stand alone gas stations that existed when the covenant was adopted in 1960. But changed conditions only operate to excuse the enforcement of a covenant if its purposes can no longer be accomplished, so the covenant will continue to be enforceable against Global.

181. The church is probably liable for a trespass. The ad coelum doctrine provides that the owner of land also owns the space above and the area below that land. The extension of the church's gutters over the store's land constituted a trespass. But the church will argue that it has adversely possessed the area occupied by the gutters. The church's gutters were there for long past the statutory period, and they were open and visible. It is unclear whether the gutters also achieved an exclusive claim to the airspace, though that seems likely. The hardest question is whether the gutters crossed the store's property under a claim of right. State courts are divided concerning the ability of an unintentional, mistaken location of a building to satisfy the claim of right requirement. Even if the church satisfied the claim of right requirement and thereby established adverse possession, the store could still argue that the falling water constitutes a trespass even if the gutters do not. That claim is doubtful, though, for it is uncertain whether the redirection of natural rainfall is a trespass, especially if the gutters that work the redirection are there lawfully.

182. The American Cancer Society owns the land. Juanita's will devised the land to the church in fee simple determinable with a shifting executory interest held by the American Cancer Society. That interest would violate the Rule against Perpetuities -except that conveyances between two charitable organizations are exempt from the Rule. The original conveyance thus remained intact. So when the school conveyed the property and the homeowner's association began to build a country club, it appears that the covenant requiring the land to be used for private Christian education has been violated. The occurrence of the stated condition caused the title to the property to shift automatically to the American Cancer Society.

183. **Answer A is the correct answer**. An easement gives its holder the right to use land owned by someone else. A right to walk across your neighbor's land is a common example of an easement. Moreover, an easement automatically transfers with the land, so the burden of the easement remained on the land when it was conveyed to the McCoys.

Answer B is incorrect because it describes a trespass by the Hatfields. The McCoys have the right to exclude others from their property, and a trespass occurs whenever anyone enters their property without the permission of the McCoys. A trespass is actionable regardless of whether the landowner suffered any actual injuries. **Answer C is incorrect** because the operation of the brick kiln constitutes a private nuisance. The fumes from the kiln have sickened the McCoys' children, which easily demonstrates that the McCoy family has suffered a substantial interference with the use and enjoyment of their land. The kiln may also constitute a public nuisance, and it is possible that it constitutes a violation of local zoning laws and state or federal environmental regulations, though there are insufficient facts to determine that here. **Answer D is incorrect** because the McCoys have a property right to be protected from subsidence, and the Hatfields will violate that right if their pool causes the subsidence.

184. **Answer D is the correct answer**. In most jurisdictions, the right to a nonconforming use does not permit the reconstruction of a building that has been destroyed, even if the destruction resulted from a natural disaster. The theory appears to be that while zoning law will tolerate the operation of existing facilities that were present before a contrary zoning provision became effective, the replacement of a facility is not entitled to the protection that zoning law grants to nonconforming uses.

Answer A is incorrect because there is no evidence that the city refused to issue the permit based upon a discriminatory motive. Standing alone, the fact that the affected families are protected from discrimination by the Fair Housing Act does not suffice, for there is no evidence that the race or national origin of the families explains the city's decision. **Answer B is incorrect** because the equal protection clause has not been interpreted to prohibit cities from limiting the number of families who live in a single house or apartment. **Answer C is incorrect** because the failure to challenge one zoning decision does not prevent a landowner from challenging future zoning decisions.

185. **Answer D is the correct answer**. Edwin & Hilles can only bring a takings claim if they can establish that they owned a property right that the government has taken from them. The closure of the walkway did not take any of the rights that the law firm owned to its own property. Instead, the only plausible claim that the firm can raise is that it obtained an implied easement that guaranteed access from its building to the stadium (and vice versa). But there is no evidence that any of the four types of implied easements were established here: there is no evidence of government misconduct that would yield an easement by estoppel; the use of the walkway was seemingly permissive and not for a long enough duration to establish an easement by prescription; and there is no indication that the land was once owned by the same person so that there could be an easement by necessity or an easement by implication.

Answer A is incorrect because courts have concluded that a sports stadium is a public use, and that issue is irrelevant here anyway. The firm's takings claim seeks compensation, and the fact that the taking was for a public use in no way eliminates the duty to pay just compensation. Likewise, **Answer B is incorrect** because the fact that the police power supports the closure of the walkway does not eliminate the compensation requirement. And, **Answer C is incorrect** because the government must pay just compensation when it takes an easement; the compensation requirement applies to most types of property interests, with the occasional exception of some future interests in land.

186. **Answer B is the correct answer.** The inscription and the fact that Lucretia had been wearing the locket suggest that she had received it as a gift from the Senator. The inscription demonstrates the intent to make the gift, and Lucretia's wearing it around her neck indicates that she accepted it. Accordingly, Lucretia is the true owner. She then lost the locket, which was found by Paula, who thus obtained good title to the locket against everyone -except Lucretia. The few days that passed, and the surreptitious way in which Paula took the locket, rebut any suggestion that Lucretia abandoned it. No bona fide purchaser exists who would defeat Lucretia's claim, so the locket belongs to her.

   Answer A is incorrect because the facts show that the Senator voluntarily gave the locket to Lucretia. **Answer C is incorrect** because Paula did not acquire good title against Lucretia, the true owner, when Paula found the locket. **Answer D is incorrect** because StuffMart was a bailee for hire for Paula, and StuffMart had no ownership claim to the locket.

187. **Answer C is the correct answer.** The government can always terminate private properties by an exercise of the power of eminent domain. Even if the sole motive of the government is to close the gas station in order to improve the residential character of the neighborhood, that interest will constitute a public use that will enable the government to purchase the property by eminent domain.

   Answer A is incorrect because the move from one use to another terminates the right to continue the nonconforming use. The switch to the video store terminated the right to the nonconforming use and was probably a violation of the zoning restrictions adopted in 2000. The fact that the city neglected to close the video store does not mean that the landowner has the right to switch back to the gas station. **Answer B is incorrect** because the storage tanks constitute a public nuisance. As such, the city will be able to enjoin the operation of the storage tanks, and it may also be able to enjoin the entire gas station as a demonstrated threat to the health of the community. **Answer D is incorrect** because the very premise of a nonconforming use is that it is out of character where it is located within the community, so the presence of lots of cars simply highlights the fact that the gas station is there as a nonconforming use instead of in compliance with the 2000 zoning restrictions.

188. **Answer C is the correct answer.** A pet is an animal that has been lawfully reduced to possession. Rhode Island's statutory change in terminology from "ownership" to "companion" does not change the ability of people to possess animals as pets.

   Answer A is incorrect because the federal Endangered Species Act prohibits anyone from possessing a listed species, such as a Florida Keys marsh rabbit, except in limited instances in which a permit is available. **Answer B is incorrect** because *Pierson v. Post*, 3 Cai. R. 175, 2 Am. Dec. 264 (N.Y. Sup. Ct. 1805) suggests that a hunter who is in hot pursuit of an animal that he or she has already wounded is deemed to have already captured that animal. Accordingly, the hunter is entitled to Bambi, and the Robinson family cannot take it from him. **Answer D is incorrect** because zoning regulations may restrict or even prohibit the presence of domesticated animals on one's land.

189. **Answer A is the correct answer**. The government can regulate a nuisance without committing a taking because a landowner's property rights never include the right to engage in a nuisance. The government cannot take something that does not belong to the landowner in the first place.

Answer B is incorrect because the injunction obligates Acme to terminate the nuisance. Closing the landfill will end the nuisance. Modifying the landfill so that it no longer interferes with the use and enjoyment of Julia's land also terminates the nuisance, which explains why **Answer C is incorrect**. **Answer D is incorrect** because Acme can negotiate with Julia by offering her enough money to settle the case. If Julia agrees, then the parties could petition the court to lift the injunction and drop the suit. In the terminology of Professors Calabresi and Malamed, that result illustrates a property right held by the plaintiff.

190. **Answer D is the correct answer**. David cannot point to any legal rule that will excuse him from paying rent. Commercial premises are rarely covered by an implied warranty of habitability. David might be able to establish a constructive eviction, but he will have to leave the premises if he wants to stop paying rent. The noise might constitute a nuisance, but the existence of a nuisance provides an independent cause of action for damages that does not excuse the affected tenant from his duty to pay rent. **Answer A is incorrect** because most states prohibit a landlord from taking any action in retaliation for a tenant asserting his or her rights. **Answer B is incorrect** because there is no evidence that the lease between Bryce and Boyd prohibited Boyd from subleasing the farmland. Courts presume that land is freely alienable unless the parties state otherwise. **Answer C is incorrect** because the failure to provide water to a residential property will violate the implied warranty of habitability that exists in nearly every state. That warranty cannot be waived, and a tenant is allowed to not pay rent but stay in possession if it is violated.

191. **Answer A is the correct answer**. The will attempted to give Andrew a life estate, to be followed by a contingent remainder in the grandchildren of Andrew who reach the age of 21. But that contingent remainder violates the Rule against Perpetuities. Andrew could have more children after Linda died, and any of those children could have their own children -Andrew's grandchildren -more than 21 years after the death of Andrew, Katy, Christina, or any other life in being at the time of Linda's death. Accordingly, the contingent remainder is struck as invalid, which leaves the devise as providing "to Andrew for life."

Answer B is incorrect because Andrew will retain the property for the duration of his life, even if Andrew has grandchildren who turn 21 while he is still alive. **Answers C and D are incorrect** because the invalidation of the contingent remainder means that the property will simply revert back to Linda's heirs once Andrew dies.

192. **Answer C is the correct answer**. The visibility of Jeff's actions from outside his property defeats any claim to the privacy of his own home that he could otherwise advance. The association will have a reasonable interest in protecting children from seeing pornographic materials.

Answer A is incorrect because there is no state action that would trigger the free speech protections of the first amendment. *Shelley v. Kraemer*, 334 U.S. 1 (1948), found state action with respect to the judicial enforcement of a racist covenant, but the courts have been unwilling to extend that decision to first amendment cases. **Answer B is incorrect** because there is an insufficient -or perhaps no -nexus between Jeff's disability as an alcoholic and his use of pornography. **Answer D is incorrect** because pornographic materials are not necessarily obscene materials, and only the possession of obscene materials can be illegal. The Supreme Court's decisions upholding municipal zoning of adult bookstores do not depend upon the obscenity of the materials there, for the zoning applied to non-obscene pornographic material as well.

193. **Answer D is the correct answer**. Intellectual property is subject to the takings clause. The government's use of property, like the company's trade secret, will always constitute a taking, no matter how important that use is to the community.

   Answer A is incorrect on either of two theories. First, the destruction of the factory could be analogized to the nineteenth century cases holding that the government need not pay compensation when it destroys buildings that are in the path of a fire that threatens to destroy the whole city. **Answer B is incorrect** because a company does not have a property right to engage in a new activity on federally owned lands. **Answer C is incorrect** because the courts have refused to hold the government responsible for the independent actions of wild animals.

194. **Answer A is the correct answer**. William's will established a joint tenancy between Paula and Lance. Lance died before the will became effective. But even if William had died before Lance, Paula would now own the farm in fee simple because of the right of survivorship contained with a joint tenancy. Paula survived Lance, so she gets the whole property.

   Answers B and C are incorrect because a joint tenant cannot devise his or her interest; that interest expires upon their death. **Answer D is incorrect** because William's will is effective notwithstanding the death of one of the named parties. For example, if William's will had devised land to Lance in fee simple, but Lance and William died in quick succession before William could change his will, then Lance's heirs would get the property. But the fact that William devised the farm as a joint tenancy means that the farm goes to the survivor of Lance and Paula, namely Paula.

195. **Answer A is the correct answer**. Like any other interest in land, a tenancy at will can be created orally if it is for a duration of less than one year. Interests in land for more than one year are subject to the Statute of Frauds, which requires that their creation be in writing.

   Answer B is incorrect because a real covenant must be in writing to be enforceable. Indeed, a reciprocal negative easement is the only example of a covenant that can be implied rather than be in writing. **Answer C is incorrect** because a homeowner's association's recreational fee is simply a type of covenant that is governed by the same rule which explains why **Answer B is incorrect. Answer**

D is incorrect because all zoning provisions -like every other legislative act -must be in writing.

196. **Answer B is the correct answer**. According to Jeremy Bentham, the most famous exponent of the utilitarian theory of property, "there is no such thing as natural property, and that is entirely the work of the law." The Visual Artists Rights Act's presumption of natural rights to certain works of art thus contradicts the utilitarian theory, which views VARA's premise as improper.

Answer A is incorrect because utilitarian theory does not say what qualifies as a socially beneficial use of land. Put differently, a utilitarian calculus could conclude that leaving land in its natural state is the most useful thing to do with that land. The Wilderness Act does just that. **Answer C is incorrect** because utilitarian theory sees all determinations of property rights as based upon subjective judgments, so the fact that local zoning decisions appear arbitrary is not troubling from a utilitarian perspective. **Answer D is incorrect** because utilitarian theory is indifferent concerning the choice of contract law principles instead of traditional property law principles. The view that the choice is subjective anyway precludes any certain choice between them.

197. **Answer B is the correct answer**. The subsistence lifestyle of the native Alaskans living near the *Exxon Valdez* oil spill was harmed by the effects of that spill. In particular, the inability of native Alaskans to use their land to provide for their subsistence qualifies as a substantial interference with the use and enjoyment of their land. As such, it is a private nuisance.

Answer A is incorrect because a fear that lacks objective scientific support will not qualify as an injury within the scope of private nuisance law. **Answers C and D are incorrect** because individuals can bring public nuisance claims only if they have suffered an injury that is different in kind from other members of the public. Here, native Alaskans are afraid of eating fish and they have lost income, but those injuries are suffered by many other Alaskans as well. Accordingly, only the government will be able to bring a public nuisance claim.

198. **Answer A is the correct answer**. A stem cell line may be patented because it is a new invention rather than a mere discovery of natural life. The patent gives Dr. Gomez a property right in the stem cell line, so **Answer B is incorrect**. Moreover, the loss of that property may be remedied in a conversion action. The facts here differ from the California Supreme Court's decision in *Moore v. Regents of the University of California*, 793 P.2d 479 (Cal. 1990), *cert. denied*, 499 U.S. 936 (1991), because the body parts at issue there were taken from a patient who did not have an expectation of retaining them after his surgery. By contrast, Dr. Gomez did have an ongoing property interest in the stem cell line that he developed, so a conversion action will be available to him. **Answers C and D are thus incorrect.**

199. **Answer D is the correct answer**. Julia failed to gain title to the doll as a gift from Laura because she refused delivery of the doll. Instead, Laura mislaid the doll that Ellen found in the trash. Ellen's title became good against everyone in the world

except Laura. In particular, Ellen's title was good against Julia, for Julia never accepted delivery of the doll as a gift from Laura. Ellen thus retained title to the doll against Julia as the finder. Ellen conveyed that title to Margaret as a bona fide purchaser because Margaret acted in good faith in purchasing the doll in the online auction.

Answer A is incorrect because Laura lost her paramount title when Margaret became a bona fide purchaser. **Answer B is incorrect** because Julia never accepted the gift. **Answer C is incorrect** because Ellen sold the doll to Margaret.

200. **Answer B is the correct answer**. Public nuisance law imposes liability upon a landowner who interferes with a right common to the general public. The theory of public nuisance law is that an owner cannot use its land in any way that causes such an injury -or the threat of such an injury -to the public. CERCLA operates from the same premise.

Answer A is incorrect because a private nuisance exists only if a particular landowner can demonstrate that it has suffered a substantial interference with the use and enjoyment of its land. That describes many but not all CERCLA cases, for CERCLA also applies to threatened releases of hazardous substances that have not yet actually occurred. Moreover, liability for a private nuisance only extends to those who cause such a nuisance, and a current landowner who had no role in depositing the substances that are found on his property may not be liable for a private nuisance. **Answer C is incorrect** because CERCLA applies to the release of substances before they actually enter someone else's property, whereas a trespass exists only when the property boundary has been crossed. CERCLA also applies to unintentional trespasses that may not result in liability under trespass law. **Answer D is incorrect** because CERCLA specifically disavowed common law negligence theories. Liability under CERCLA is strict; indeed, proof of causation is not required. Negligence principles only apply once CERCLA liability is established and each party's relative share of the cleanup costs is being determined.

201. **Answer D is the correct answer**. Most jurisdictions will allow a landlord to refuse to agree to a tenant's proposed assignment for any -or no -reason if the lease contains a provision prohibiting assignments. Some jurisdictions no longer follow that rule with respect to residential leases, but a no-assignment provision in a commercial lease like that here will be enforceable.

Answer A is incorrect because Stacy wants to transfer her entire remaining interest in the property, which makes the transfer an assignment within the meaning of the original lease agreement. **Answer B is incorrect** because neither a tenant's general appearance nor a tenant's tattoos in particular constitutes a protected characteristic under the Fair Housing Act. **Answer C is incorrect** because at least some jurisdictions maintain that a landlord cannot condition the approval of an assignment upon the tenant's paying any excess rent to the landlord.

202. **Answer D is the correct answer**. Under any recording statute, Emily has better title than the Van Burens because she was the first purchaser for value to record

her deed. Hugh obtained good title from Emily once she was the true owner by virtue of her recording her deed.

Answer A is incorrect because LADC conveyed away its title -twice. **Answer B is incorrect** because the Van Burens failed to record their deed before Emily, who was a purchaser for value, so the Van Burens lose to Emily under any recording statute. **Answer C is incorrect** because Emily conveyed good title to Hugh.

203.   **Answer B is the correct answer**. The Court's opinion repeatedly emphasized that the village government was entitled to determine the appropriate pattern of land uses within the community. The Court declined to completely abdicate any judicial oversight over local land use decisions, but the Court deferred to the reasonable conclusions of the village government even when others strenuously objected to them.

Answer A is incorrect because the Court did not conduct an independent review of the record, and it did not find that the company's proposed use of its land was not "otherwise safe and innocent." Indeed, the Court spent little time discussing Amber Realty's actual plans, focusing instead upon the zoning ordinance as a whole. **Answer C is incorrect** because the Court reaffirmed that the due process clause, and implicitly the takings clause, operate to limit municipal land use decisions even if those decisions are intended to provide for the public good. **Answer D is incorrect** because the Court did not address Ambler Realty's contentions concerning what constitutes beauty, choosing to defer to the village government's more generalized conclusions about land use instead.

204.   **Answer A is the correct answer**. Single-family homes that are sold or rented by their owners are exempt from the Fair Housing Act, provided that the owners do not use a realtor or own more than three rental properties. Thus, a homeowner can discriminate based upon race or any other protected characteristic as far as the FHA is concerned.

Answer B is incorrect because the FHA does not allow a benevolent motive to excuse decisions based upon race or any other protected characteristic. **Answer C is incorrect** because the FHA covers advertising for housing as well as the actual sale and rental of housing. **Answer D is incorrect** because the FHA prohibits discrimination based upon religion, again notwithstanding any desire to create a particular kind of community.

205.   **Answer A is the correct answer**. Jill obtained the student loans before she got married, so they will be treated as separate property rather than marital property. Community property laws govern the equal distribution of marital property; the rule is the same for liabilities as it is for assets.

Answers B and C are incorrect because the credit card debt and the mortgage were each acquired while Jill and Jack were married, so they will be treated as marital property. **Answer D is incorrect** because Jill's ongoing ownership interest in the house will probably protect her from having to pay rent to Jack to live in it. Only if Jill has acted to exclude Jack will she then have an obligation to pay him rent.

206.   **Answer C is the correct answer**. A covenant will be judged abandoned if the parties whom it benefits have frequently declined to enforce it. The fact that 22 residents operate businesses out of their homes notwithstanding the presence of an identical covenant against such businesses suggests that the covenant has been abandoned. Alternately, laches or estoppel could prevent the enforcement of the covenant.

   Answer A is incorrect because the mere possibility that the city council might change the area's zoning to commercial does not provide sufficient evidence that conditions in the neighborhood have changed so dramatically to justify the termination of the covenant. **Answer B is incorrect** because the presence of other residential developments in no way obligates a resident to move from Brady Village to make way for other uses. **Answer D is incorrect** because the relative value of the properties does not demonstrate changed conditions -for the disparity may have always existed -and it does not make the covenant enforceable.

207.   **Answer D is the correct answer**. Esther apparently mislaid the watch in the Dickens grocery store. As such, the store has a better claim to the watch than Cara, who found it on the store's counter. Cara, however, sold the watch to Betsy. But Betsy does not appear to be a good faith purchaser: she joined the police, Cara, and the store in trying to search for the original owner. Thus Betsy did not acquire title to the watch against the store, which had the superior right to Cara.

   Answer A is incorrect because Andy cannot gain good title to the watch by the criminal act of theft. **Answer B is incorrect** because Betsy was not a good faith purchaser. **Answer C is incorrect** because the watch was mislaid and thus becomes the property of the store pending the discovery of the true owner. If the watch had been lost by Esther, say by dropping it under some boxes in the corner of the store, then Cara would gain better title than the store.

208.   **Answer C is the correct answer**. Helga induced Oscar to believe that the Audubon Society would be able to use her land for the upcoming annual conventions. Oscar then invested extensive time and resources into the planning for the convention, only to learn that Helga had changed her mind. In other words, Helga misled Oscar, who acted in reliance upon Helga's misrepresentation, and Oscar will be injured if he cannot use Helga's land as she initially promised. Helga is estopped from claiming that the convention is trespassing on her land.

   Answer A is incorrect because an express easement is an interest in land that is subject to the Statute of Frauds, which requires that any interest in land of more than one year's duration be in writing. **Answer B is incorrect** because there was no common ownership of the land, and there is no real necessity to use the land. **Answer D is incorrect** because Oscar and the convention participants do have a right to use Helga's land by virtue of an easement by estoppel.

209.   **Answer A is the correct answer**. The federal Fair Housing Act (FHA) prohibits housing discrimination based upon race, religion, sex, and other criteria. The effect of such a prohibition on discrimination is to expand the pool of potential homeowners and tenants beyond what it would be if discrimination were allowed to continue. That

larger pool of homeowners and tenants will create market pressures for more housing, which developers will exploit by building more units. The only objection to this reasoning is that developers will not build housing for disfavored groups regardless of the FHA's commands, but the number of developers who are so intent upon discriminating and violating the law is likely to be far smaller than the number of developers who will build more housing.

Answer B is incorrect because state statutes protecting wildlife habitat, like many other environmental protections, operate to increase the cost of land. Such regulations reduce the amount of land upon which housing can be built, but the demand for housing will be unchanged, so the demand will push cost of the smaller supply of land higher. **Answer C is incorrect** because local zoning ordinances containing minimum lot size requirements have the same effect as regulations protecting wildlife habitat: they reduce the supply of land for housing and thus increase its cost. **Answer D is incorrect** because a warranty of habitability increases the costs imposed upon landlords without any expectation that tenants will be able to afford those costs. Developers will be discouraged from building additional housing units subject to such higher maintenance costs but no higher income.

210.   **Answer B is the correct answer**. Matthew prevails because he recorded his deed first. The fact that he knew of the earlier conveyance to Jennifer does not matter under a race statute.

Answer A is incorrect because the common law rule gives the land to Jennifer as the first party to acquire the property from SDC. **Answers C and D are incorrect** because the notice provisions of both a notice statute and a race-notice statute preclude Matthew from gaining better title than Jennifer when he knew that she had already obtained the property from SDC.

211.   **Answers B is the correct answer**. The courts have upheld restrictions on the number of **unrelated** people living in an apartment or in a **single-family** home. But the restriction in Answer B does not refer to "more than two **unrelated** people;" it simply refers to "more than two people." That restriction will thus be likely to fail as an interference with constitutional protections of the family under the fourteenth amendment, and perhaps (though less likely) as a violation of the federal Fair Housing Act's prohibitions on discrimination based upon family status as well.

Answer A is incorrect because the Supreme Court has upheld municipal regulations on the proximity of adult bookstores provided that alternative venues exist in the community. A 25-year amortization period is sufficient to allow any existing, nonconforming uses to recover their costs before the ordinance requires them to move or close. **Answer C is incorrect** because while New Jersey and some other states have identified state constitutional restrictions on such exclusionary zoning, most states have not interfered with such municipal zoning decisions even when they have an adverse effect on the poor and on racial minorities. **Answer D is incorrect** because it simply describes the ordinance contested in **Village of Euclid v. Ambler Realty Co.**, 272 U.S. 325 (1926). Municipalities are given broad discretion to determine which uses are allowed in which zones.

212. **Answer C is the correct answer**. Juan gave Angela a fee simple subject to an executory interest with that executory interest held by Bob's widow. That executory interest satisfies the Rule against Perpetuities. To be sure, "Bob's widow" was not ascertained at the time of the conveyance: the law presumes that Bob could divorce Elizabeth, remarry someone else who was not even alive at the time of the conveyance, and leave his young second wife as his widow. But the executory interest held by "Bob's widow" must vest or fail by the time that Angela dies. If the property is not developed during Angela's lifetime, then her heirs get to keep it upon her death. In other words, the executory interest will vest and become possessory if the property is developed during her lifetime, but that interest will fail and never become possessory if the property is undeveloped when Angela dies. Therefore, the executory interest must either vest or fail at the time of Angela's death, and the unknown identity of "Bob's widow" does not matter to the validity of the interest.

    Answer A is incorrect because the validity of the executory interest means that Angela does not hold the property in fee simple absolute. **Answer B is incorrect** because the future interest created by Juan is an executory interest rather than a right of reentry, so the fee simple conveyed to Angela is subject to that executory interest. **Answer D is incorrect** because Angela does gain an interest in the property from Juan, and she would do so regardless of the validity of the interest conveyed to Bob's widow and his heirs.

213. **Answer B is the correct answer**. Janice and CT Realty created a tenancy at will when Janice began paying rent and CT Realty allowed her to live in the apartment. A tenancy at will last until either of the parties provides notice that they want to terminate the estate. CT Realty's request for Janice to leave will end the lease and obligate Janice to vacate the premises.

    Answer A is incorrect because the actions of the parties created a tenancy at will that allows Janice to stay until the landlord asks her to leave. **Answer C is incorrect** because CT Realty retains the right to terminate the lease at any time upon adequate notice, so Janice does not have a right to stay even if she is willing to continue paying the rent. **Answer D is incorrect** because the parties did not state a specific term for the lease, so a tenancy at will was established. The fact that Janice hoped to live there for the school year did not give her the right to do so.

214. **Answer B is the correct answer**. The agreement between Calvin and Donna was a sublease because it was for less than the entire estate owned by Calvin. Accordingly, Lucy can sue Calvin for rent, so **Answers C and D are incorrect.** **Answer A is incorrect** because Lucy can also evict Donna, but most states will prevent Lucy from suing Donna for rent because Lucy and Donna are not in privity of contract or estate.

215. **Answer C is the correct answer**. An invention is not entitled to a patent if the invention was "obvious." This requirement serves to reinforce the purpose of the patent power to reward creativity, for there is no creativity in making something that was already obvious to others.

Answer A is incorrect because the failure to challenge the issuance of a patent does not preclude collateral attacks on the patent in a later infringement proceeding. **Answer B is incorrect** because the mere fact that someone thought of an invention does not affect the ability of another person to obtain a patent for that invention once it is actually developed. **Answer D is incorrect** because while the common law refused to provide exclusive rights to inventors, Congress decided otherwise and the Patent Act does provide such exclusive rights for a limited time.

216. **Answer C is the correct answer.** It is unclear whether the Islamic Center will prevail on any of these theories. Even so, RLUIPA is the most likely to result in a favorable decision for the Islamic Center. The public testimony suggesting that "there are enough of these people around here anyway" could be construed to voice popular hostility against Muslims in the community, though that statement is capable of other interpretations as well. If a judge decides that the statement provides evidence of religious discrimination, then the town would have the burden of demonstrating a compelling state interest in the denial of the permit. The conclusory assertion that the government is best situated to provide services to the homeless is unlikely to be viewed as sufficiently compelling.

Answer A is incorrect because the police power grants a town broad authority to engage in zoning, including zoning of religious uses and zoning of the location of non-profit services. **Answer B is incorrect** because the Fair Housing Act only applies to housing discrimination, not to the kind of discrimination in providing food to the poor that is alleged here. **Answer D is incorrect** because the free exercise clause requires greater evidence of purposeful discrimination than RLUIPA, and the free exercise clause does not demand that the government justify its decisions with a compelling state interest.

217. **Answer C is the correct answer**. Riparian rights attach depending upon the proximity of a landowner to the river, lake, or other body of water. The use of the water is governed by rules that generally require each owner of riparian land to act reasonably. Riparian rights, therefore, exist irrespective of whether the water has been captured or possessed.

Answer A is incorrect because wild animals become property only once they are captured and reduced to possession, as illustrated by **Pierson v. Post**, 3 Cai. R. 175, 2 Am. Dec. 264 (N.Y. Sup. Ct. 1805). **Answer B is incorrect** because most states provide that natural gas does not become property until it is removed from the ground or otherwise controlled by a surface landowner or a party acting with permission to drill at the site. **Answer D is incorrect** because the law of prior appropriation distributes rights to water in most western states depending upon who used that water first.

218. **Answer A is the correct answer**. A machine can be destroyed by whoever owns it. Whether or not the machine was produced by a patented process does not affect the right to destroy the machine itself. In the same way, a copyrighted book may be thrown in the trash. The point is that it is the intellectual property right that is protected, not the particular manifestation of it.

Answer B is incorrect because the federal Visual Artists Recognition Act prohibits the destruction of certain works of art. **Answer C is incorrect** because many state statutes and local historic preservation ordinances protect historic buildings from being modified, let alone destroyed. **Answer D is incorrect** because the status of a pet as personal property does not entitle its owner to destroy it; local animal cruelty statutes will prevent such an action.

219.   **Answer D is the correct answer**. The best hope for the residents of the retirement community is to bypass the village council and try to amend the zoning law by a direct vote of the people of the village. Popular initiatives are a common means of enacting zoning amendments. That tactic might be successful here because it is unlikely that a majority of the residents of the village approve of a land use scheme designed solely for the benefit of the mayor.

       Answer A is incorrect because a shopping center does not constitute a nuisance, no matter where it is located. **Answer B is incorrect** because the authority for zoning laws under the state's police power is well established. **Answer C is incorrect** because the government has not taken the land of the retirement community, nor has it used their land, nor has it regulated their land. The issuance of a government permit for an unwanted activity will not constitute a taking of the neighboring land, save perhaps in an extraordinary case where the government literally permits a nuisance.

220.   **Answer B is the correct answer**. Many older decisions, and a handful of more recent ones, affirm that sights and sounds that are offensive to a reasonable member of a community can serve as the basis for a nuisance action. The fact that Betty has required medical treatment makes it even more likely that the injury she experienced will suffice to state a nuisance claim. For the same reason, **Answer C is incorrect**. **Answer A is incorrect** because a nuisance action can succeed even if the objectionable activity has received a governmental permit, or if it occurs in a place where zoning law allows. Similarly, **Answer D is incorrect** because the government's decision not to enforce a regulation governing the objectionable conduct does not preclude a private nuisance suit. A private party can sue regardless even if the administrative agency has determined that no violation has occurred, for the courts retain the power to independently adjudicate nuisance claims.

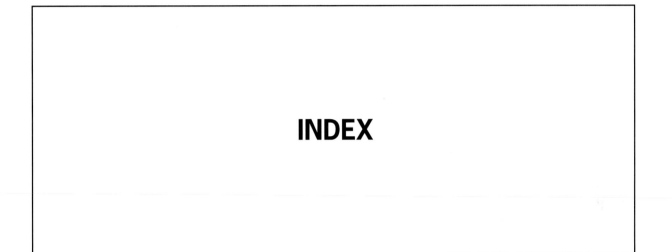

INDEX

INDEX

TOPIC | **QUESTION**

Accession 9, 103

Accretion 9, 102

Ad coelum doctrine 101, 104, 162, 181

Adverse possession 25, 99, 105, 106, 157, 181

Animals 10, 33, 37, 107, 188, 217, 218, 220

Avulsion 9, 102

Bailments 24, 25, 29, 186

Bona fide purchasers 14, 20, 21, 27, 199, 207

Concurrent ownership

    Concurrent ownership — Estates 65, 66, 68, 70, 73, 75, 178, 194

    Concurrent ownership — Marital property 3, 61, 64, 65, 66, 67, 68, 71, 72, 74, 205

    Concurrent ownership — Rights of cotenants 69, 73, 74, 178

Easements 147, 183

    Easements — Conservation easements 112, 116, 130

    Easements — Scope 112, 125, 126, 130

Eminent domain power 95, 147, 161, 169, 187

Estates of land

    Estates of land — Future interests 42, 43, 44, 45, 46, 47, 48, 49, 50, 51, 52, 53,

TOPIC   **QUESTION**

54, 55, 56, 58, 59, 60,
61, 62, 63, 171, 179,
182, 191, 212

Estates of land — Leasehold 83, 86, 88, 91, 95, 96,
105, 195

Estates of land — Present estates 42, 43, 44, 45, 46, 47,
48, 49, 50, 51, 55, 57,
58, 60, 61, 62, 171,
179, 182, 191, 194,
212

Estates of land — Rule against Perpetuities 46, 47, 49, 50, 51, 52,
53, 54, 56, 59, 61, 171,
179, 182, 191, 212,
213

Finders 3, 6, 13, 17, 18, 22,
25, 186, 207

Gifts 15, 16, 19, 25, 26, 28,
174, 199

Growth controls 137, 176

Housing codes   93

Housing discrimination 76, 94, 97, 132, 177,
184, 192, 201, 204,
209, 216

Humans and body parts 30, 32, 35, 40, 198

Intellectual property 8, 23, 38

Intellectual property — Copyrights 34, 39, 41, 218

Intellectual property — Patents 36, 215, 218

Intellectual property — Right of publicity 3, 175

Intellectual property — Trade secrets 35, 193

Intellectual property — Trademarks 6, 11, 31, 37, 39, 164

TOPIC	QUESTION
Landlord/tenant	196, 213
Landlord/tenant — Assignments	87, 201
Landlord/tenant — Constructive eviction	92
Landlord/tenant — Delivery of possession	84, 89
Landlord/tenant — Estates	83, 86, 88, 91, 95, 96, 105, 195
Landlord/tenant — Illegal lease doctrine	77
Landlord/tenant — Landlord rights	89, 95, 190, 214
Landlord/tenant — Quiet enjoyment	92
Landlord/tenant — Subleases	87, 190, 201
Landlord/tenant — Tenant rights	78, 85, 90, 190
Landlord/tenant — Warranty of habitability	80, 82, 85, 92, 209
Mistaken improvers	9, 103
Nuisance law	
Nuisance law — Private nuisances	113, 122, 147, 162, 163, 183, 189, 197, 200, 219, 220
Nuisance law — Public nuisances	150, 187, 197, 200
Property	
Property — Meaning of property	1, 4, 7, 155, 161
Property — Property rights	5, 8, 11, 120
Property — What constitutes property	2, 10, 23, 172, 196
Public lands	4, 6, 136, 153, 196
Public trust doctrine	7, 138
Public housing	209

TOPIC	**QUESTION**
Recording of deeds	98, 100, 106, 108, 202, 210
Rent controls	79, 81
Servitudes	7, 110, 114
Servitudes — Creation	117, 121, 124, 129, 195
Servitudes — Enforcement of covenants	110, 111, 119, 121, 123, 129, 131, 180, 192, 206
Takings	146, 155
Takings — Eminent domain power	95, 147, 161, 169, 187
Takings — Just compensation	165, 169
Takings — Public use	160, 166, 185
Takings — What constitutes a taking	154, 155, 157, 158, 159, 162, 163, 164, 166, 167, 168, 169, 170, 176, 185, 193, 219
Theories of property	11
Theories of property — Economic	11
Theories of property — Labor	6, 11
Theories of property — Natural law	8, 11, 173
Theories of property — Occupation	3
Theories of property — Utilitarian	4, 30, 136, 196
Trespass	101, 106, 107, 109, 181, 183, 200
Water rights	12, 217

TOPIC   **QUESTION**

Zoning 5, 134, 147, 172, 196, 203, 209

Zoning — Aesthetic zoning 133, 135, 149

Zoning — Amendments 143, 172, 206, 219

Zoning — Comprehensive plans 143, 150

Zoning — Conditional rezoning 139, 150

Zoning — Conditional uses 132

Zoning — Constitutional limits 145, 148, 149, 184, 203, 211, 216, 219

Zoning — Floating zones 152

Zoning — Nonconforming uses 140, 142, 146, 184, 187

Zoning — Special exceptions 141, 146

Zoning — Spot zoning 6, 7, 139

Zoning — Variances 144, 146, 162, 195